The New Wine and Soul Survivor Songbook

passion

for

your

name

Compilation Copyright © New Wine (Chorleywood) Ltd. 1995.
First Published 1995.

No part of this publication may be reproduced in any form, or by any means, **including photocopying** and translation, without permission in writing from the publishers.

We apologise for any omissions in this edition
and will do our best to put them right in future editions.

The quotations from the Bible on 'blank' pages are from the Holy Bible: New International Version, Copyright © International Bible Society 1973, 1978 & 1984.
Published by Hodder & Stoughton Ltd. and used by permission.

Produced and edited by David Mitchell.

Published by:
New Wine (Chorleywood) Ltd,
37, Quickley Lane,
Chorleywood,
Herts WD3 5AE.
(01923) 446655

ISBN 0-9524430-1-5

Printed in Great Britain by I.P.A. Print Associates Limited, Chesham, Bucks.

Dear Friends,

Once again we are delighted to welcome you to the New Wine and Soul Survivor songbook.

This year's edition contains many fresh songs which are used at the conferences, including all those on Matt's Redman's album "Passion For Your Name." Other authors include David Ruis, Flamme, Kevin Prosch, Jeff Searles and Martin Smith. A large number of the songs are previously unavailable as published sheet music. At the end of the book you will find a set of acetate masters for all Matt Redman's songs.

We hope this book will be a valuable resource for you and your church.

Yours in Christ,

David Pytches   Mike Pilavachi

Editor's Note:
I have attempted to make this songbook as practical as possible. Each song is fully arranged for piano and tries, as best as possible, to reflect the appropriate feel. Additionally, with many of the songs where the writer is a guitarist, the "authentic" chords have been included. Therefore, on occasion, the guitar chords are a variation of the written piano chord. I would like to thank Louisa Thomas, Steve Cantellow and Matt Redman for their assistance in producing this songbook.

Yet a time is coming
And has now come
When the true worshippers
Will worship the Father
In spirit and truth,
For they are the kind of
Worshippers the Father seeks.

John 4: 23.

Contents

Sheet Music

	Song no:
Better is one day	*11*
Can I ascend	1
Come, fire of God	*34*
Come, Spirit, come	2
Did you feel the mountains tremble	3
Don't let my love grow cold	4
Down the mountain	5
Father of creation	6
Filled with Your joy	7
Fill us up and send us out	*9*
For He is worthy	*26*
Friend of sinners	8
Gloria	*31*
Have you not said	9
How long	10
How lovely is Your dwelling place	11
I ask for freedom	12
I could sing unending songs	13
I have come to love You	14
I know Your arms are open wide	15
I'm coming up the mountain	*1*
I remember the day	16
It's rising up	17
I've found Jesus	*32*
I was a lost soul	18
I will offer up my life	19
I will worship	20

	Song no:
Jesus, is this song of love	21
Kiss the Son	*35*
Let Your fire burn in me	22
Let Your glory fall	*6*
Light the fire again	*4*
My Jesus I love thee	23
Rags to riches	24
Remember	*16*
Sons and daughters	*12*
Shout to the Lord	25
Shout to the Lord	26
Sing a song of celebration	27
Surely the time has come	*33*
The cross has said it all	28
The happy song	*13*
The river is here	*5*
They that wait on the Lord	29
This means I love You	30
Turned me around	*18*
Wash me and make me Yours	31
Well, I hear they're singing	32
We've had a light	33
We will dance	*27*
When Your spirit and Your fire	34
When You've been broken	35
You are worthy of my praise	*20*

Acetate Masters for Matt Redman's songs.

1. Can I Ascend
I'm Coming Up The Mountain

Matt Redman
Psalm 24: 3,4
Exodus 33

Can I asc- end the hill of the Lord? Can I stand in that ho- ly place? There to ap- proach the glo- ry of my God; Come to- wards to seek Your face. Pur- i- fy my heart and pur- i- fy my hands. For I know it is on ho- ly ground I'll stand.

Copyright © 1995 Kingsway's Thankyou Music, PO Box 75, Eastbourne, East Sussex, BN23 6NW, UK.
Used by permission.

Copyright © 1995 Kingsway's Thankyou Music, PO Box 75, Eastbourne, East Sussex, BN23 6NW, UK.
Used by permission.

— un-veiled be-fore You, I will come.

I'm com-ing to wor-ship, I'm com-ing to bow down,

I'm com-ing to meet with You.

Repeat as required

Chords Used In This Song

A Dsus2/G D Em G D/F# Dsus4/F#

Copyright © 1995 Kingsway's Thankyou Music, PO Box 75, Eastbourne, East Sussex, BN23 6NW, UK.
Used by permission.

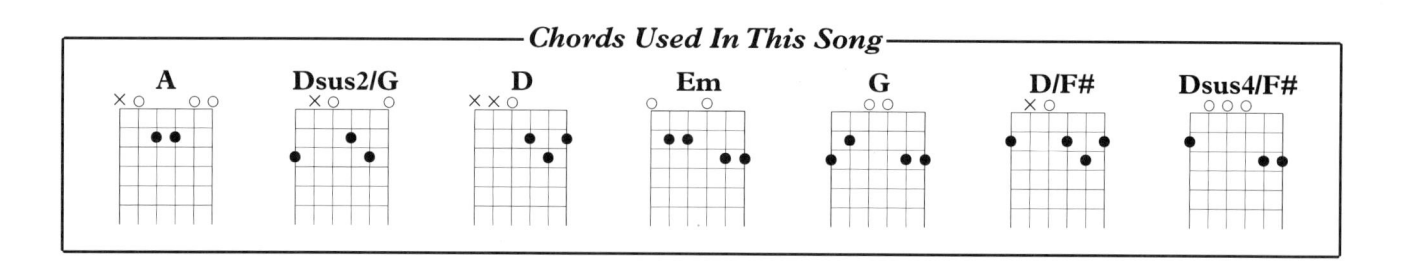

Who may ascend the hill of the Lord?
Who may stand in His holy place?
He who has clean hands
And a pure heart . . .

Psalm 24: 3,4.

2. Come, Spirit, Come

Elizabeth Bourbourze
Translation: Judith Robertson

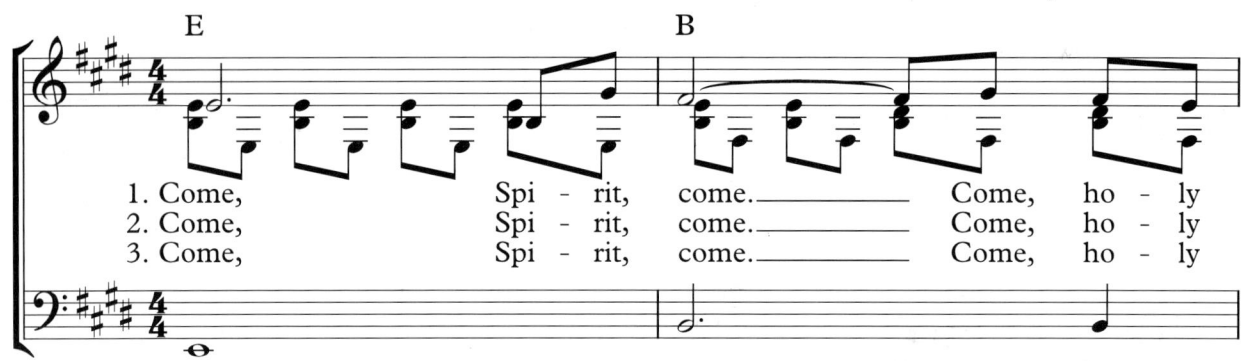

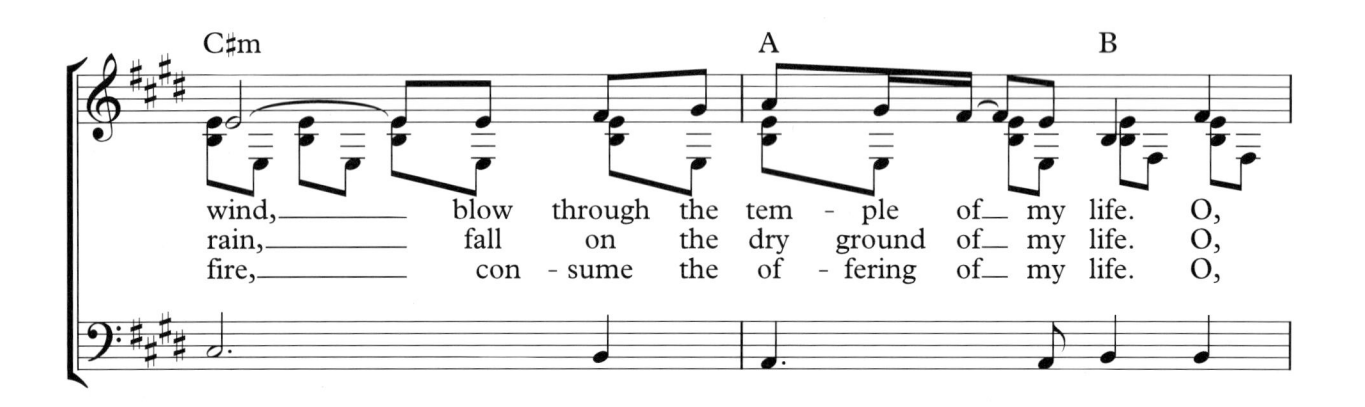

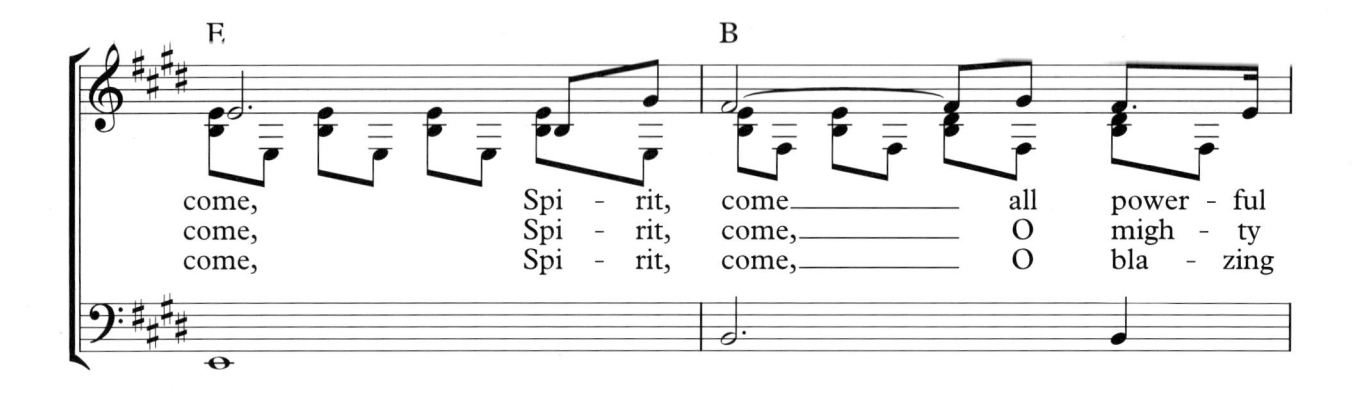

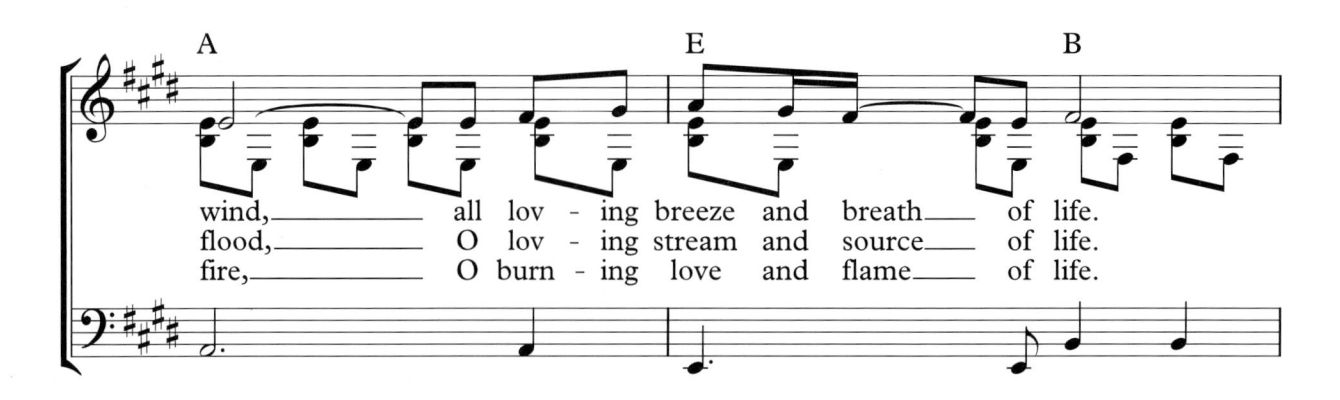

1. Come, Spirit, come. Come, holy wind, blow through the temple of my life. O, come, Spirit, come all power-ful wind, all lov-ing breeze and breath of life.

2. Come, Spirit, come. Come, holy rain, fall on the dry ground of my life. O, come, Spirit, come, O might-y flood, O lov-ing stream and source of life.

3. Come, Spirit, come. Come, holy fire, con-sume the of-fering of my life. O, come, Spirit, come, O blazing fire, O burn-ing love and flame of life.

Copyright © 1994 Elizabeth Bourbouze/LTC, 92 rue Rebeval, 75019 Paris, France.
Used by permission.

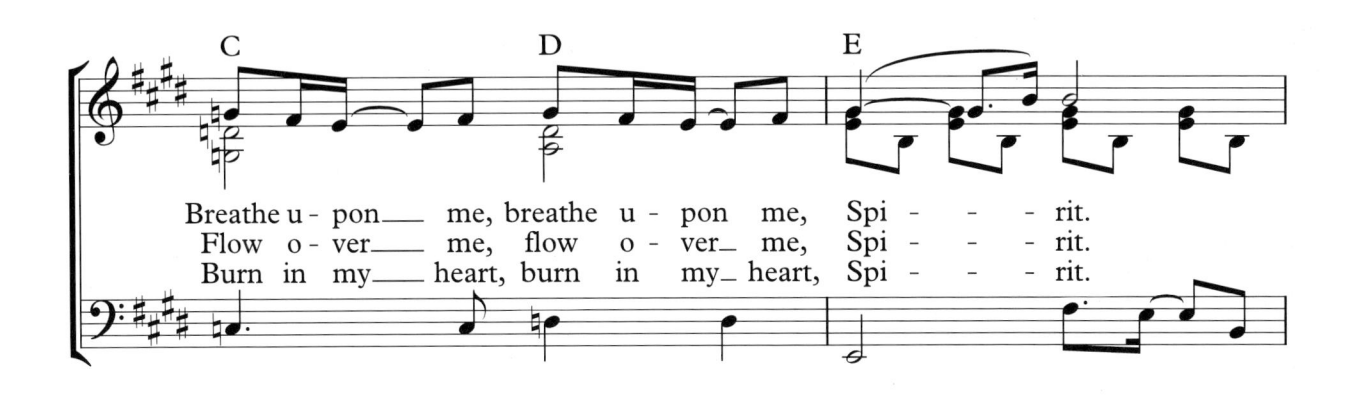

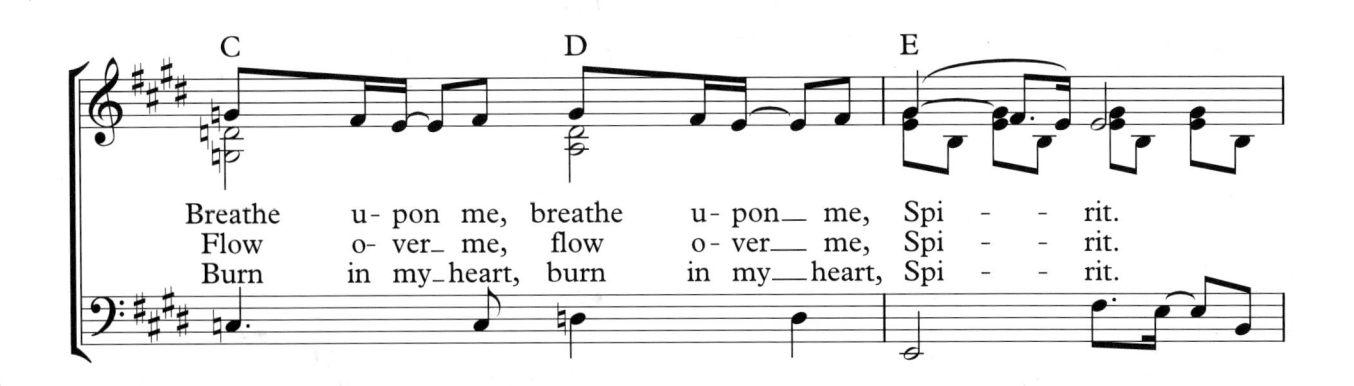

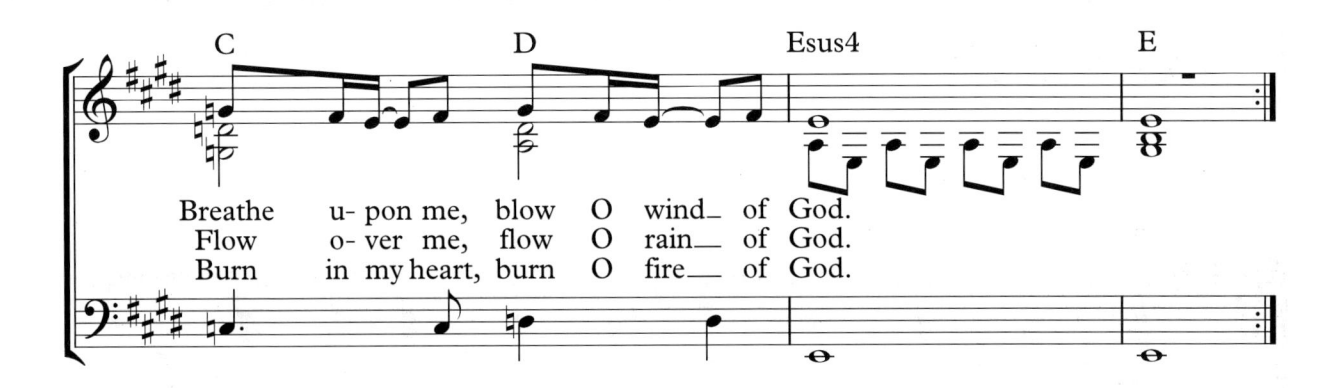

Breathe upon me, breathe upon me, Spirit.
Flow over me, flow over me, Spirit.
Burn in my heart, burn in my heart, Spirit.

Breathe upon me, breathe upon me, Spirit.
Flow over me, flow over me, Spirit.
Burn in my heart, burn in my heart, Spirit.

Breathe upon me, blow O wind of God.
Flow over me, flow O rain of God.
Burn in my heart, burn O fire of God.

Copyright © 1994 Elizabeth Bourbouze/LTC, 92 rue Rebeval, 75019 Paris, France.
Used by permission.

3. Did You Feel The Mountains Tremble

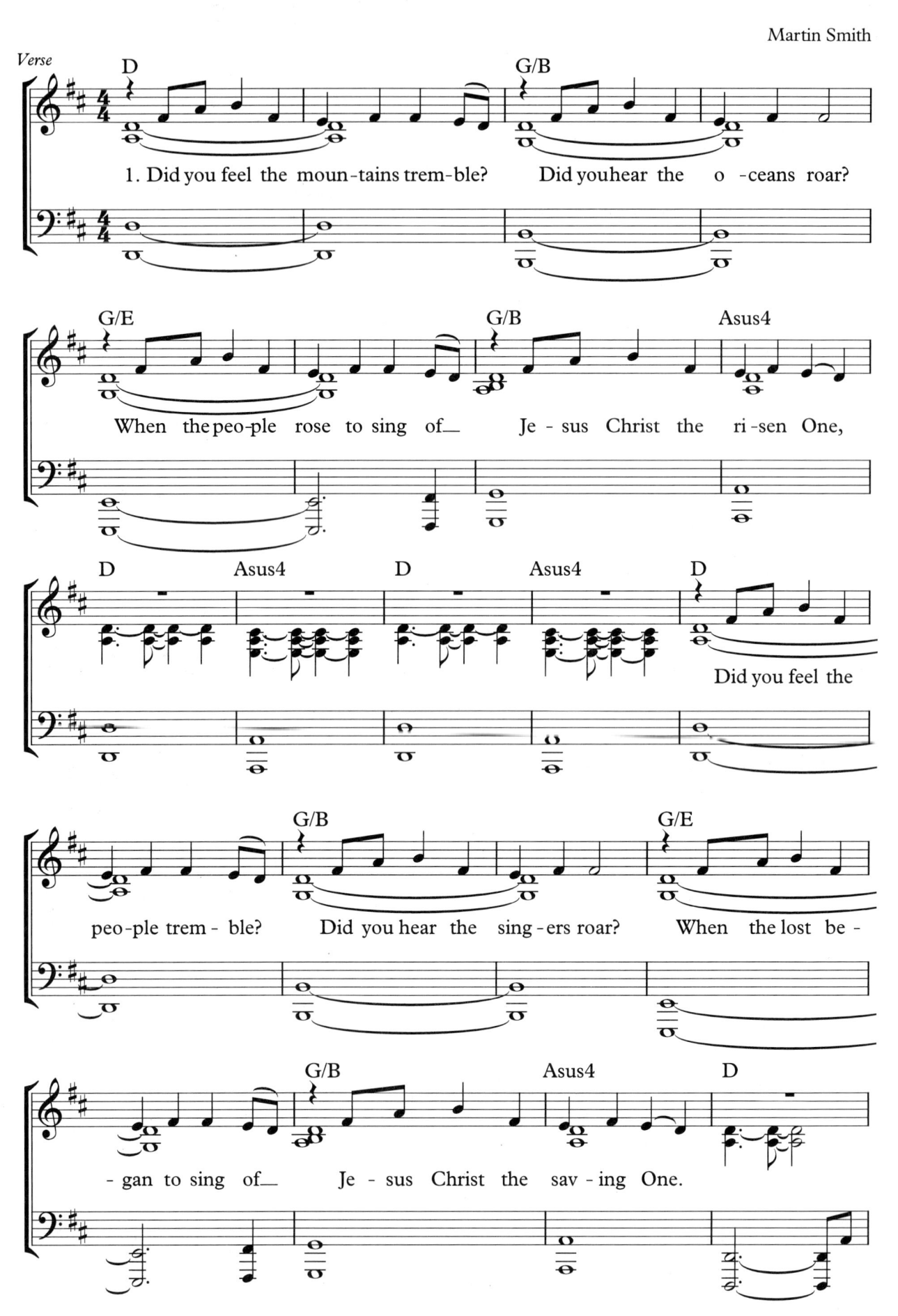

Martin Smith

Verse

1. Did you feel the mountains tremble? Did you hear the oceans roar? When the people rose to sing of Jesus Christ the risen One,

Did you feel the people tremble? Did you hear the singers roar? When the lost began to sing of Jesus Christ the saving One.

Copyright © 1994 Curious? Music U.K./Kingsway's Thankyou Music, PO Box 75, Eastbourne, East Sussex, BN23 6NW, UK. Used by permission.

And we can see that God You're moving. A mighty river through the nations. And young and old will turn to Jesus. Fling wide you heavenly gates, prepare the way of the risen Lord.

Chorus
Open up the doors and let the music play, let the streets resound with

Copyright © 1994 Curious? Music U.K./Kingsway's Thankyou Music, PO Box 75, Eastbourne, East Sussex, BN23 6NW, UK. Used by permission.

sing - ing. Songs that bring Your hope, songs that bring Your joy, dan - cers who dance upon in - just - ice.

Verse
2. Do you feel the dark - ness trem - ble, when all the saints join in one song? And all the streams flow as one ri - ver, to wash a - way our bro - ken - ness. And here we see that God Your mov

Copyright © 1994 Curious? Music U.K./Kingsway's Thankyou Music, PO Box 75, Eastbourne, East Sussex, BN23 6NW, UK.
Used by permission.

-ing. A time of jub-i-lee is com-ing. When young and old re-turn to Je-sus. Fling wide you heav-en-ly gates. Pre-pare the way of the ri-sen Lord.

Ending

Chords Used In This Song

D   G/B   G/E   Asus4

TUNE BOTTOM E DOWN TO D

The music for Martin Smith's other songs can be obtained by telephoning: 01903 733031

Copyright © 1994 Curious? Music U.K./Kingsway's Thankyou Music, PO Box 75, Eastbourne, East Sussex, BN23 6NW, UK.
Used by permission.

4. Don't Let My Love Grow Cold
Light The Fire Again

Capo 3 (D)

Brian Doerksen

Don't let my love grow cold, I'm calling out, light the fire again. Don't let my vision die, I'm calling out, light the fire again

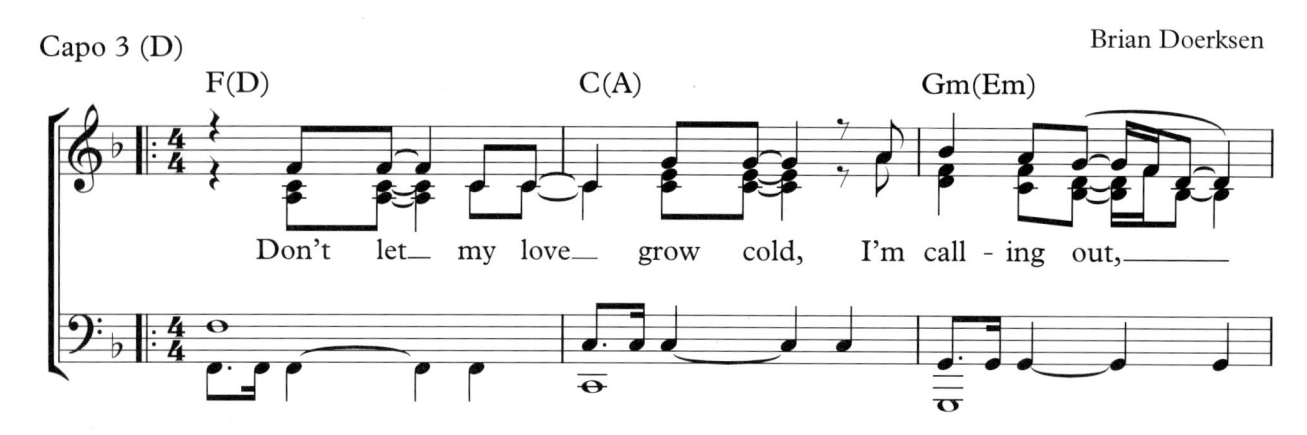

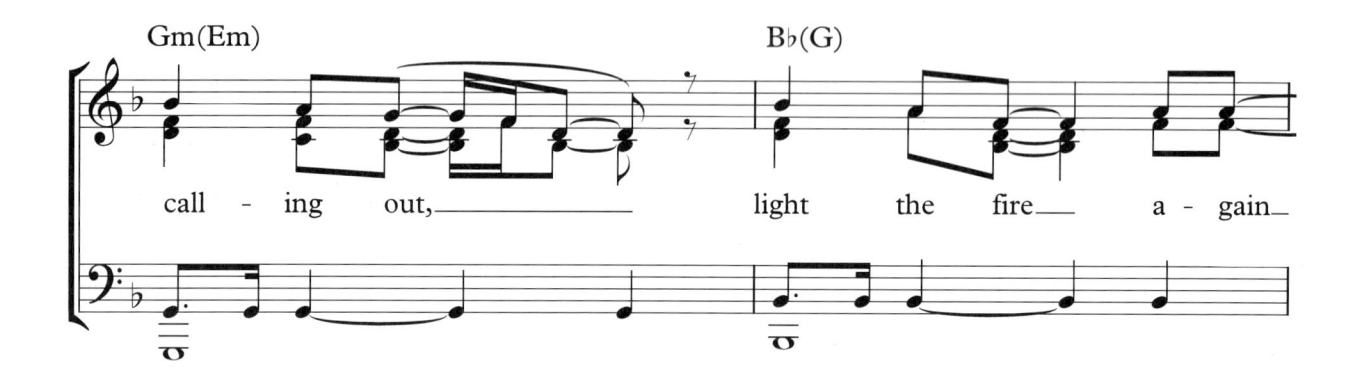

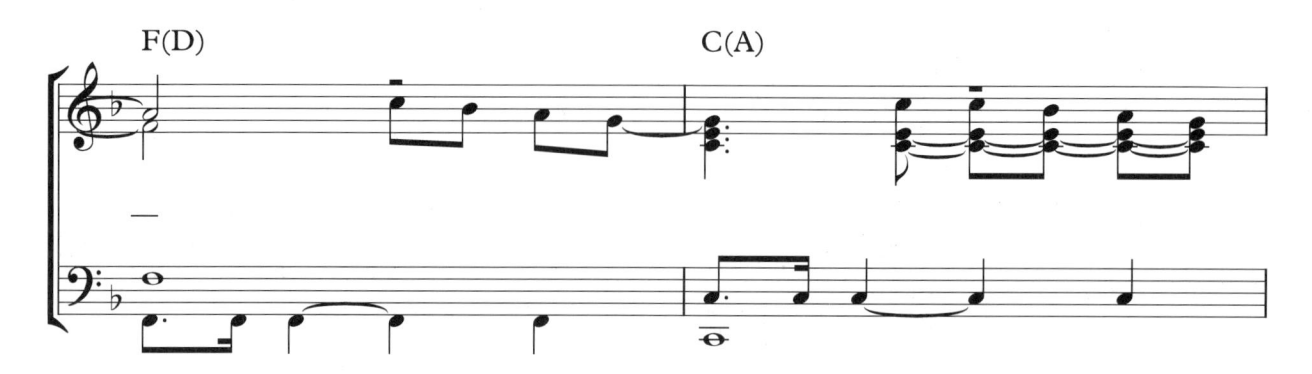

Copyright © 1994 Mercy Publishing/Kingsway's Thankyou Music, PO Box 75, Eastbourne, East Sussex, BN23 6NW, UK.
Used by permission.

You know my heart, my deeds, I'm calling out, light the fire again. I need Your dis-ci-pline, I'm calling out, light the fire a-gain.

Last time end

I am here to buy gold, re-fined in the fire; nak-

Copyright © 1994 Mercy Publishing/Kingsway's Thankyou Music, PO Box 75, Eastbourne, East Sussex, BN23 6NW, UK.
Used by permission.

-ed and poor, wretch-ed and blind, I come. Clothe me in white, so I won't be a-shamed: Lord, light the fire a-gain.

I counsel you to buy from me
Gold refined in the fire . . .

Revelation 3: 18.

5. Down The Mountain
The River Is Here

Andy Park

Intro

Verse

1. Down the mountain the river flows, and it brings refreshing wher-
3. to the mountain we love to go, to find the presence

-ever it goes. Through the valleys and over the fields, the
of the Lord. A-long the banks of the river we run, we

river is rushing and the river is here. The
dance with laughter giving praise to the Son.

Chorus

river of God sets our feet a-dancing, the river of God fills our

---

Copyright © 1994 Mercy Publishing/Kingsway's Thankyou Music, PO Box 75, Eastbourne, East Sussex, BN23 6NW, UK.
Used by permission.

hearts with cheer; the ri-ver of God fills our mouths with laugh-ter, and
we re-joice for the ri-ver is here.

2nd time to v3.
Last time end

2. The
3. Up

Verse
ri-ver of God is teem-ing with life and all who touch it can
be re-vived, and those who lin-ger on this ri-ver's shore will

To chorus
come back thirst-ing for more of the Lord. The

Copyright © 1994 Mercy Publishing/Kingsway's Thankyou Music, PO Box 75, Eastbourne, East Sussex, BN23 6NW, UK.
Used by permission.

6. Father Of Creation
Let Your Glory Fall

David Ruis

Intro

Verse

1. Father of creation, unfold Your sov'reign plan
2. Ruler of the nations, the world has yet to see

Raise up a chosen generation that will march through the land.
the full release of Your promise, the church in vict'ry.

All of creation is longing
Turn to us Lord and touch us,

Copyright © 1993 Mercy Publishing/Kingsway's Thankyou Music, PO Box 75, Eastbourne, East Sussex, BN23 6NW, UK.
Used by permission.

for Your un-veil-ing of pow'r.
make us strong in Your might.

Would You re-lease Your a-noin-ting,
Ov-er-come our weak-ness

oh God let this be the hour.
that we could stand up and fight.

Chorus
Let Your glo-ry fall in this room, let it go forth from here to the na-tions. Let Your fragrance rest in this place, as we gath-er to seek Your

Copyright © 1993 Mercy Publishing/Kingsway's Thankyou Music, PO Box 75, Eastbourne, East Sussex, BN23 6NW, UK.
Used by permission.

Copyright © 1993 Mercy Publishing/Kingsway's Thankyou Music, PO Box 75, Eastbourne, East Sussex, BN23 6NW, UK.
Used by permission.

Be exalted O God,
Above the heavens;
Let your glory be over all the earth.

Psalm 57: 5.

8. Friend Of Sinners

Matt Redman

1. Friend of sinners, Lord of truth, I am falling in love with You.
2. Friend of sinners, Lord of truth, I am giving my life to You.

Chorus
Friend of sinners, Lord of truth, I have fallen in love with You.
Friend of sinners, Lord of truth, I have given my life to You.
Jesus, I love Your name, the name by which we're saved. Jesus, I love Your name, the name by which we're saved.

Copyright © 1994 Kingsway's Thankyou Music, PO Box 75, Eastbourne, East Sussex, BN23 6NW, UK.
Used by permission.

9. Have You Not Said
Fill Us Up and Send Us Out

Matt Redman
Isaiah 43
Acts 1:8

1. Have You not said as we pass through water You will be with us? And You have said when we walk through fire we will not be burned. We are not afraid, for You are with us, we will testify to the honour of Your name. We are witnesses— You have shown us You are the One who can

Copyright © 1995 Kingsway's Thankyou Music, PO Box 75, Eastbourne, East Sussex, BN23 6NW, UK.
Used by permission.

Copyright © 1995 Kingsway's Thankyou Music, PO Box 75, Eastbourne, East Sussex, BN23 6NW, UK.
Used by permission.

Bring them from a-far, all the nations, from the north and south draw-ing all the peo-ples in. Cor-ners of the earth, come to see there's on-ly one Sa-viour and King.

To chorus

Chords Used In This Song

G   C   D   Am7   Em7

Copyright © 1995 Kingsway's Thankyou Music, PO Box 75, Eastbourne, East Sussex, BN23 6NW, UK.
Used by permission.

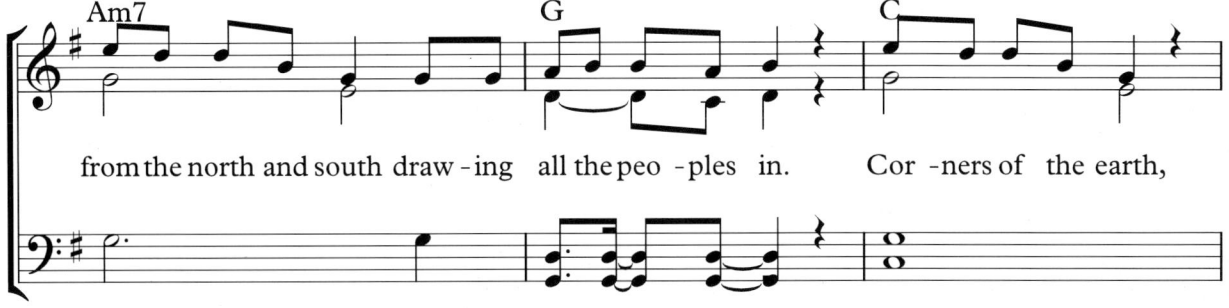

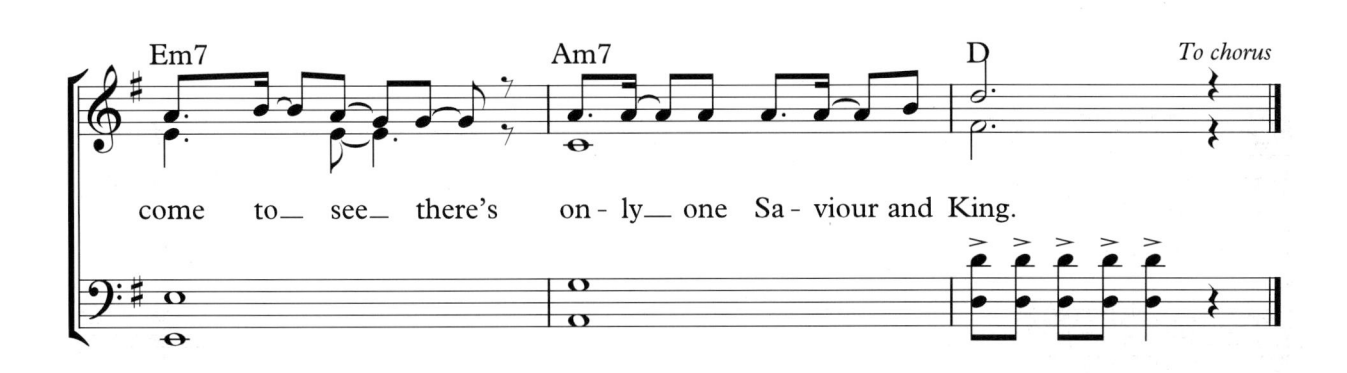

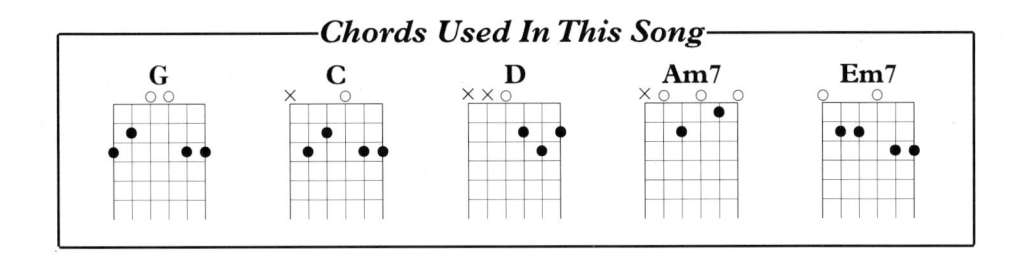

10. How Long

Jeff Searles

Verse

1. How long has it been since I felt ___ Your wind blow a-cross my face? How long has it been since I've stood ___ in Your house and known Your lo-ving grace? How long? How long has it been since I've stood ___ u-pon the land and seen the power of Your hand?

Copyright © 1995 Big Bright Sky Music, 340 Patricia Drive, San Luis Obispo, Ca. 93410, USA.
Used by permission.

Copyright © 1995 Big Bright Sky Music, 340 Patricia Drive, San Luis Obispo, Ca. 93410, USA.
Used by permission.

E
How long has it been since I've known the truth that You're al - ways

A2 **Bsus4**
___ near? How long?

E
How long has it been since I've poured out my-self__ be-fore Your

A2 **E**
Throne of__ Grace? How long has it been since I've gi-

A2
-ven my love__ be-fore I've come with my ne-eds?__

Bsus4 *To chorus*
How long?

Copyright © 1995 Big Bright Sky Music, 340 Patricia Drive, San Luis Obispo, Ca. 93410, USA.
Used by permission.

11. How Lovely Is Your Dwelling Place
Better Is One Day

Matt Redman
Psalms 27, 63 & 84

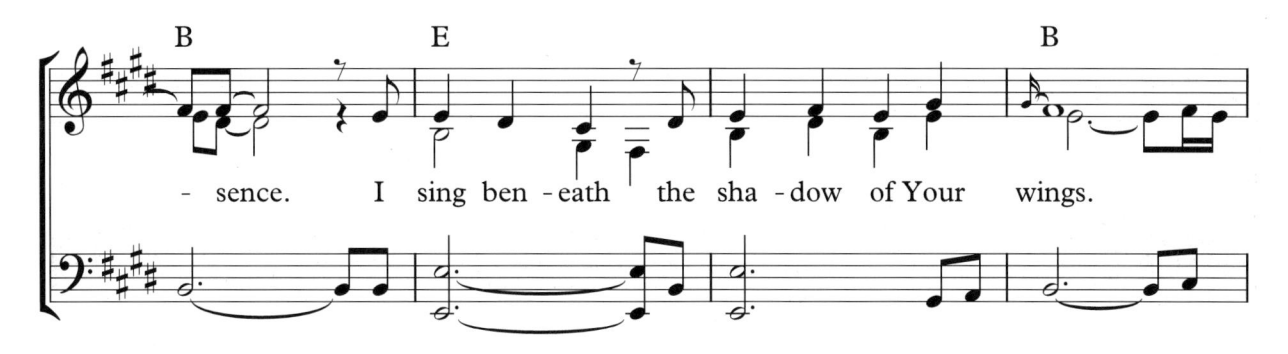

Verse

1. How lovely is Your dwelling place, O Lord Almighty.
My soul longs and even faints for You.
For here my heart is satisfied, within Your presence.
I sing beneath the shadow of Your wings.

Copyright © 1995 Kingsway's Thankyou Music, PO Box 75, Eastbourne, East Sussex, BN23 6NW, UK.
Used by permission.

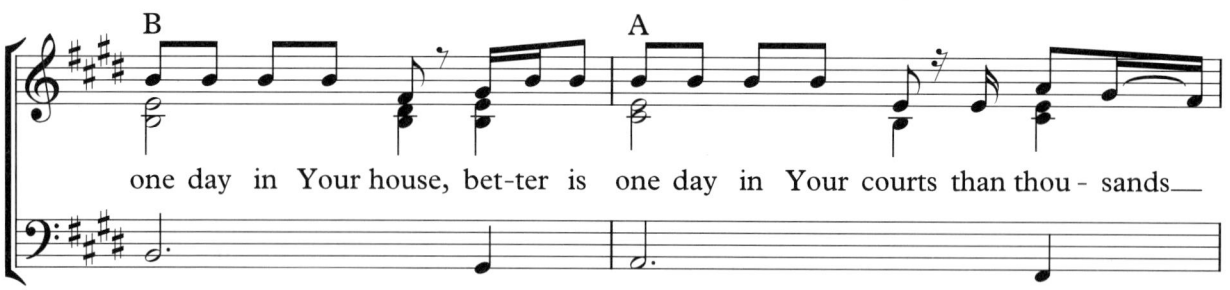

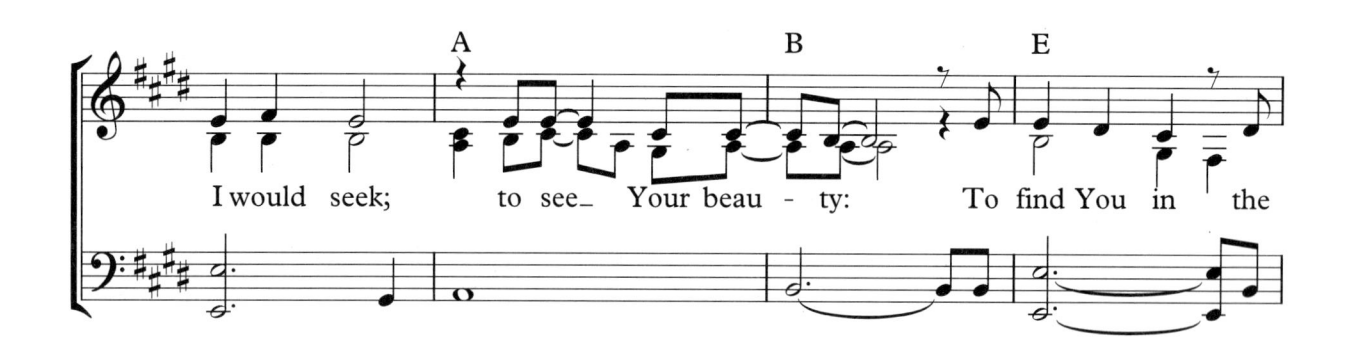

Copyright © 1995 Kingsway's Thankyou Music, PO Box 75, Eastbourne, East Sussex, BN23 6NW, UK.
Used by permission.

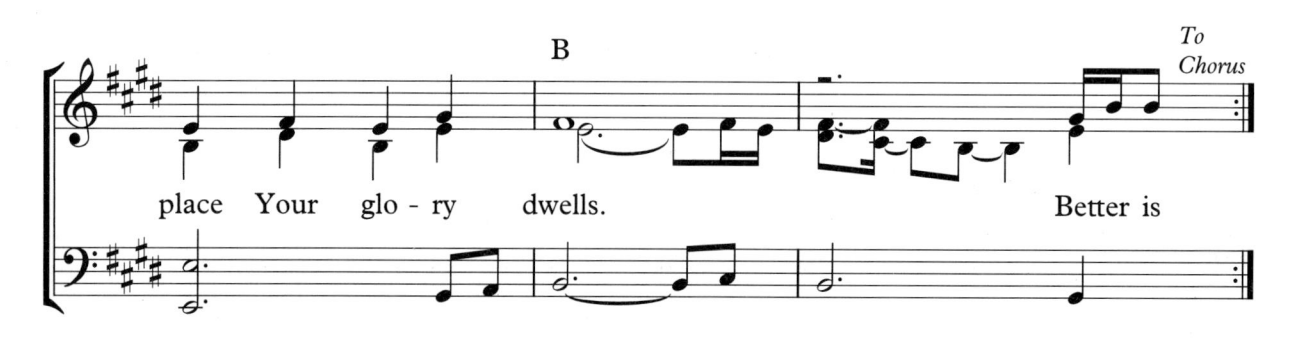

Bridge

My heart and flesh cry out for You, the liv-ing God.

Your Spi-rit's wa-ter for my soul. I've tas-ted and I've seen,

come once a-gain to me; I will draw near to You,

I will draw near to You. Bet-ter is

Chords Used In This Song

Copyright © 1995 Kingsway's Thankyou Music, PO Box 75, Eastbourne, East Sussex, BN23 6NW, UK.
Used by permission.

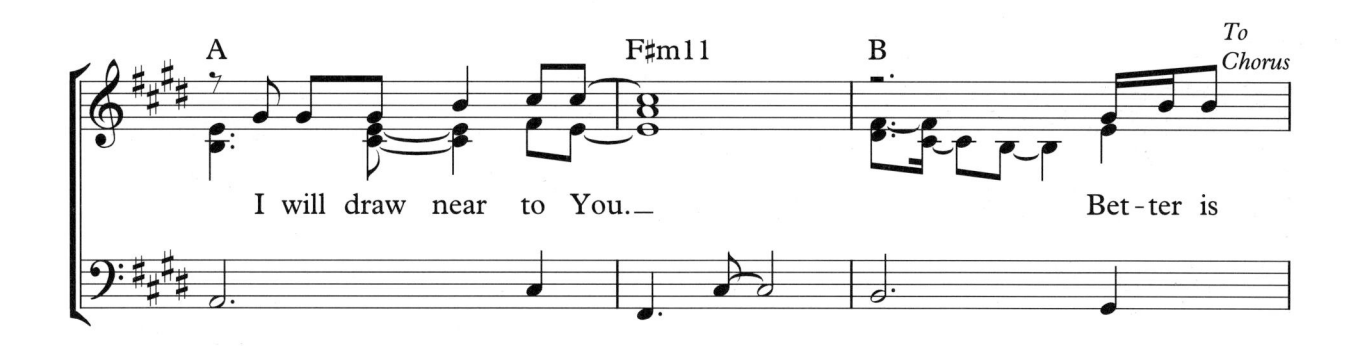

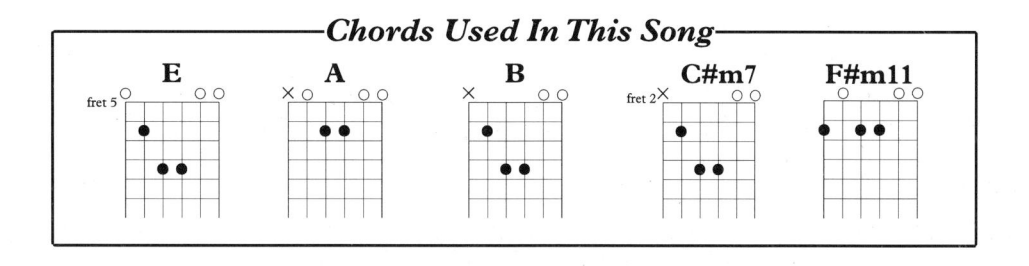

12. I Ask For Freedom
Sons and Daughters

David Ruis

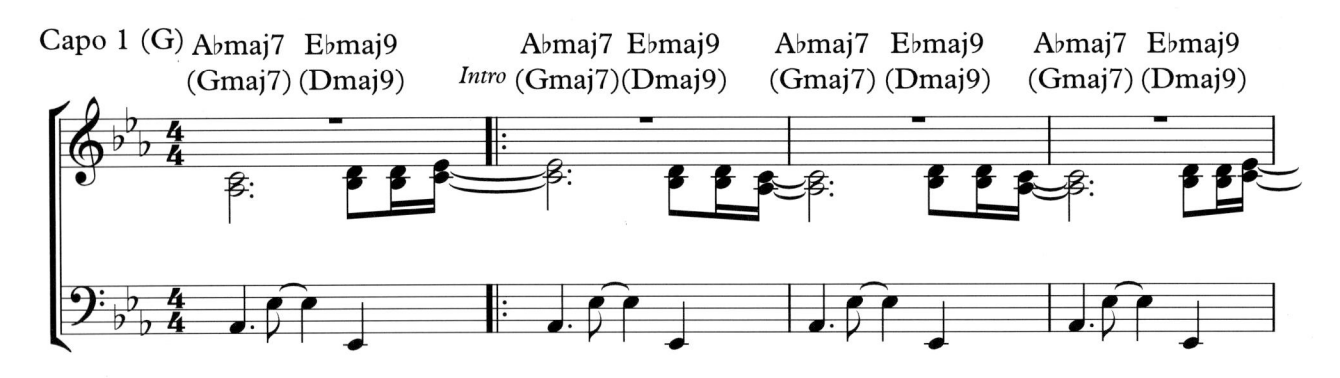

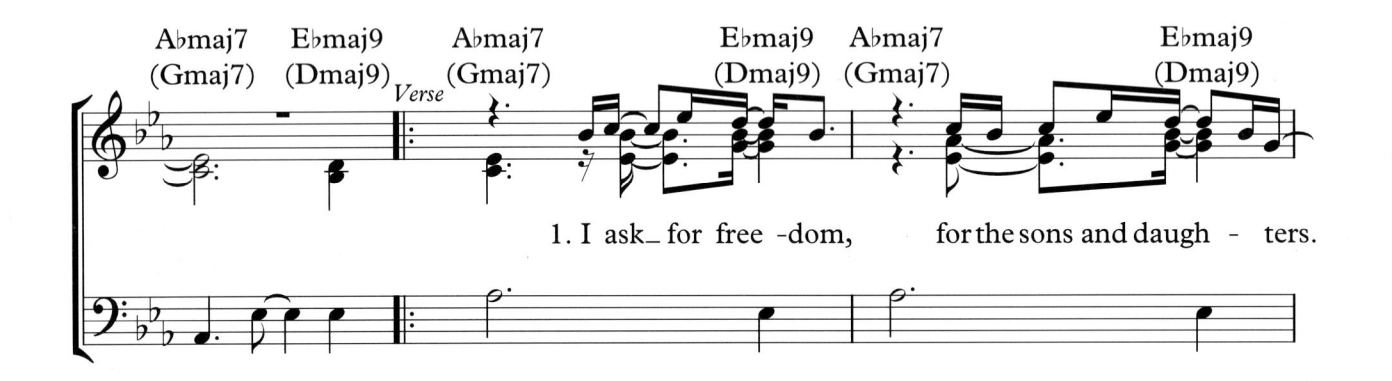

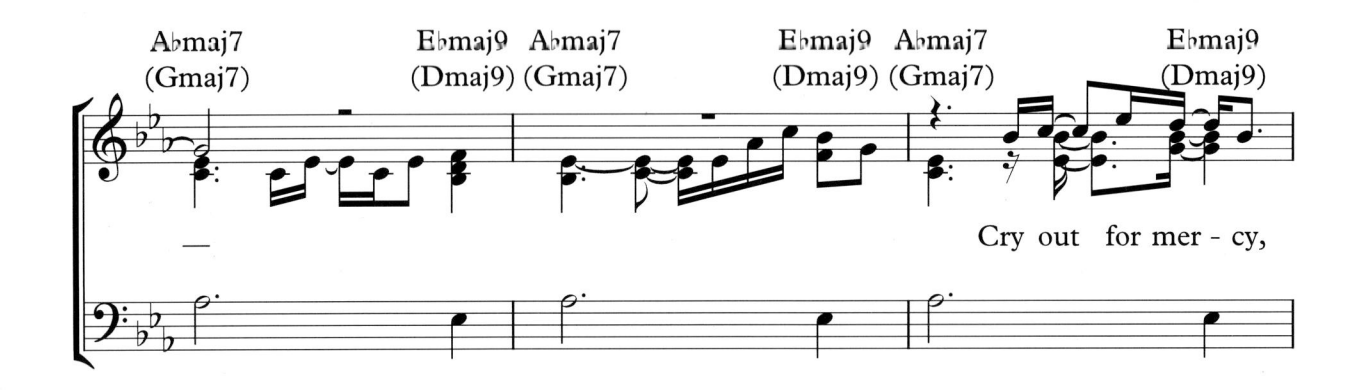

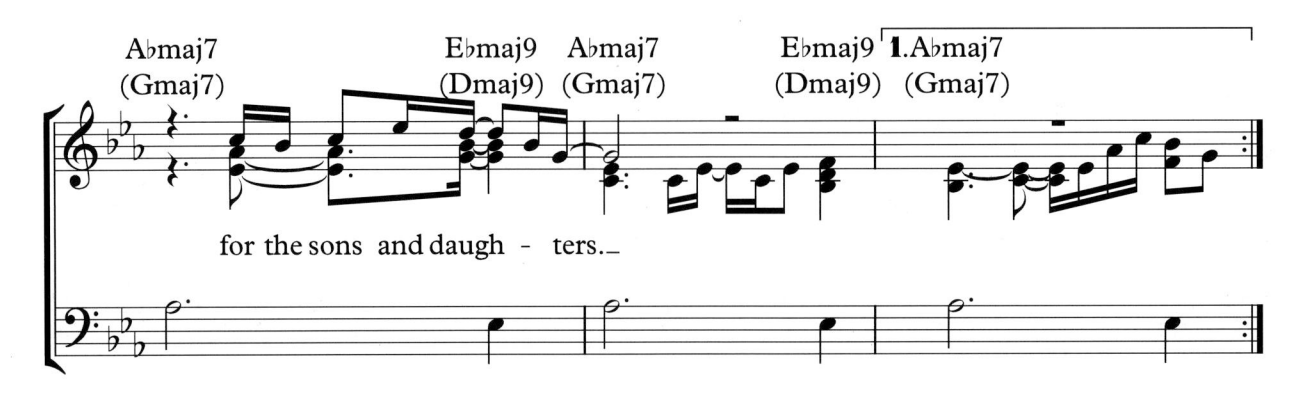

Capo 1 (G)

1. I ask for freedom, for the sons and daughters.

Cry out for mercy,

for the sons and daughters.

Copyright © 1995 Orchard Shade, 90 Noble Avenue, Winnipeg, Mb R2L0J6, USA.
Used by permission.

Copyright © 1995 Orchard Shade, 90 Noble Avenue, Winnipeg, Mb R2L0J6, USA.
Used by permission.

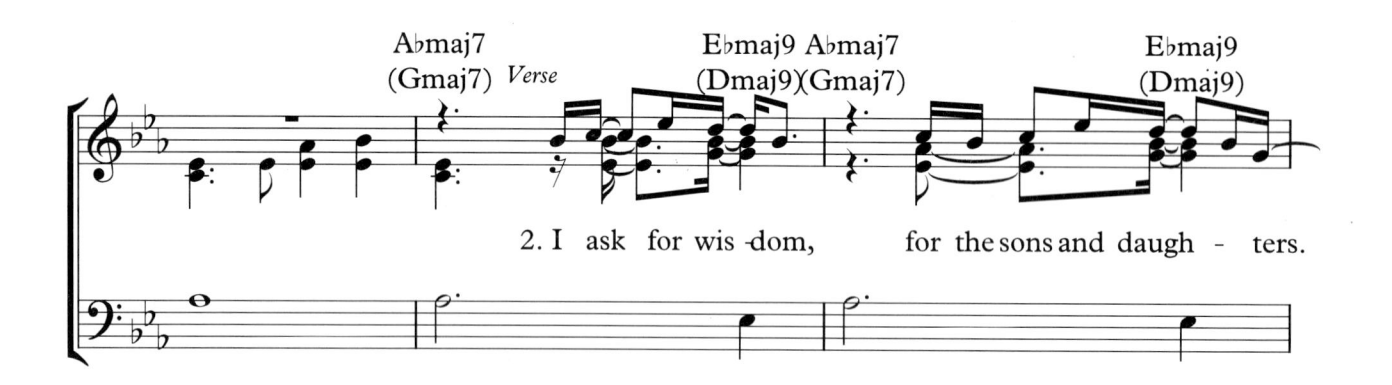

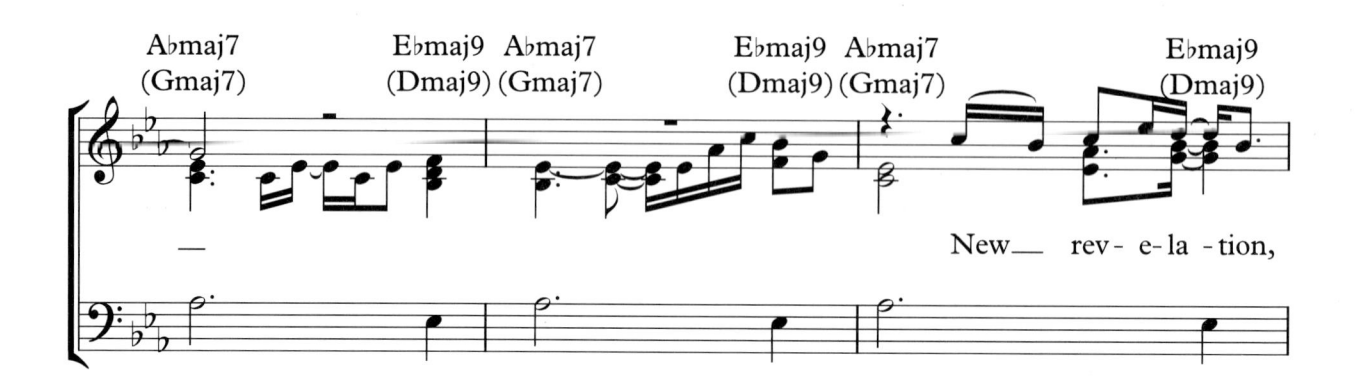

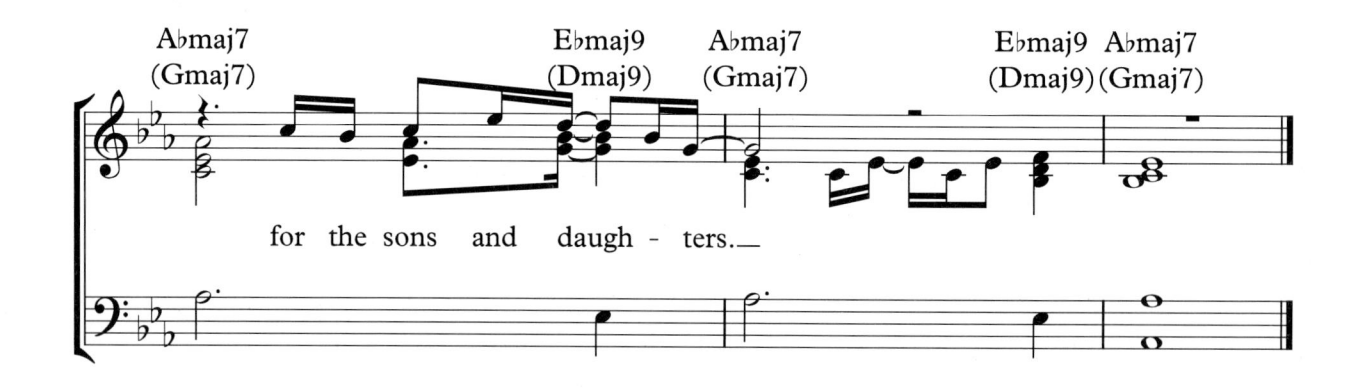

find the one that's clos- er than bro-ther to trust.

2. I ask for wis-dom, for the sons and daugh-ters.

New revelation,

for the sons and daugh-ters.

Copyright © 1995 Orchard Shade, 90 Noble Avenue, Winnipeg, Mb R2L 0J6, USA.
Used by permission.

13. I Could Sing Unending Songs
The Happy Song

Martin Smith

Oh, I could sing un-end-ing songs of how You saved my soul. Well, I could dance a thou-sand miles be-cause of Your great love.

2nd time to bridge

My heart is burst-ing Lord. To tell of all You've done. Of how You changed my life and wiped a-way the past.

Copyright © 1994 Curious? Music U.K./Kingsway's Thankyou Music, PO Box 75, Eastbourne, East Sussex, BN23 6NW, UK. Used by permission.

I wan-na shout it out. From eve-ry roof top sing. For now I know that God is for me not a-gainst me.

Bridge
Eve-ry-bod-y's sing-ing now, 'cos we're so happy! Eve-ry-bod-y's dan-cing now, 'cos we're so hap-py. If on-ly we could see Your face and see You smi-ling o-ver us and un-seen an-gels cel-e-brate,

Copyright © 1994 Curious? Music U.K./Kingsway's Thankyou Music, PO Box 75, Eastbourne, East Sussex, BN23 6NW, UK.
Used by permission.

for joy is in this place!

Oh,

To continue / To beginning / To end

Chords Used In This Song

G D/F# Em7 Csus2 D G/B Am

The music for Martin Smith's other songs can be obtained by telephoning: 01903 733031

Copyright © 1994 Curious? Music U.K./Kingsway's Thankyou Music, PO Box 75, Eastbourne, East Sussex, BN23 6NW, UK.
Used by permission.

14. I Have Come To Love You

Matt Redman

Capo 2 (A)

Verse

1. I have come to love You, I have come to love You to-day.
2. I have come to wor-ship, I have come to wor-ship to-day.
3. I have come to thank You, I have come to thank you to-day.

I have come to love You, I have come to love You to-day.
I have come to wor-ship, I have come to wor-ship to-day.
I have come to thank You, I have come to thank You to-day.

Chorus

I have come to love You to-day. And to day
I have come to wor-ship to-day.
I have come to thank You to-day.

and for-ev-er more I'll love Your name.

Lord, to-day and for ev er more I'll love Your name.

Copyright © 1995 Kingsway's Thankyou Music, PO Box 75, Eastbourne, East Sussex, BN23 6NW, UK.
Used by permission.

15. I Know Your Arms Are Open Wide

Matt Redman
Inspired by redemption hymns of
W. Spencer Walton and D. Jenkins

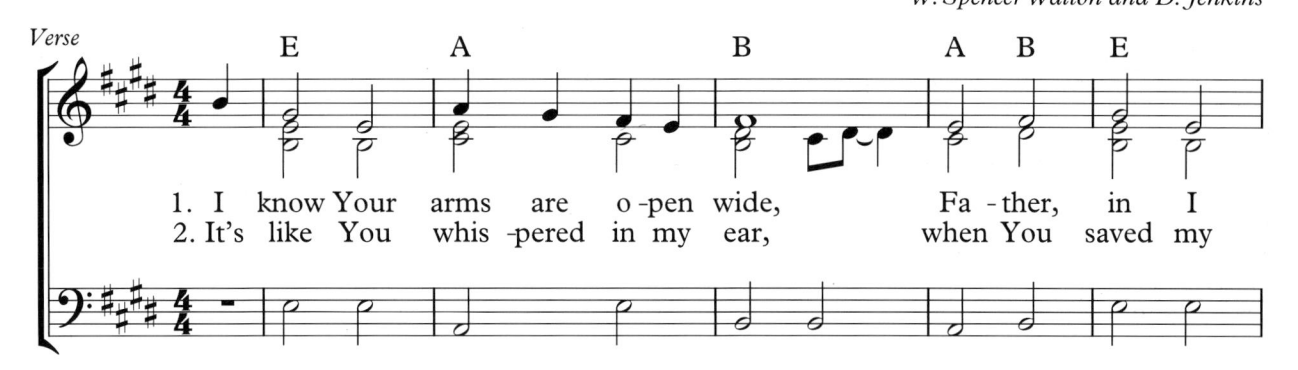

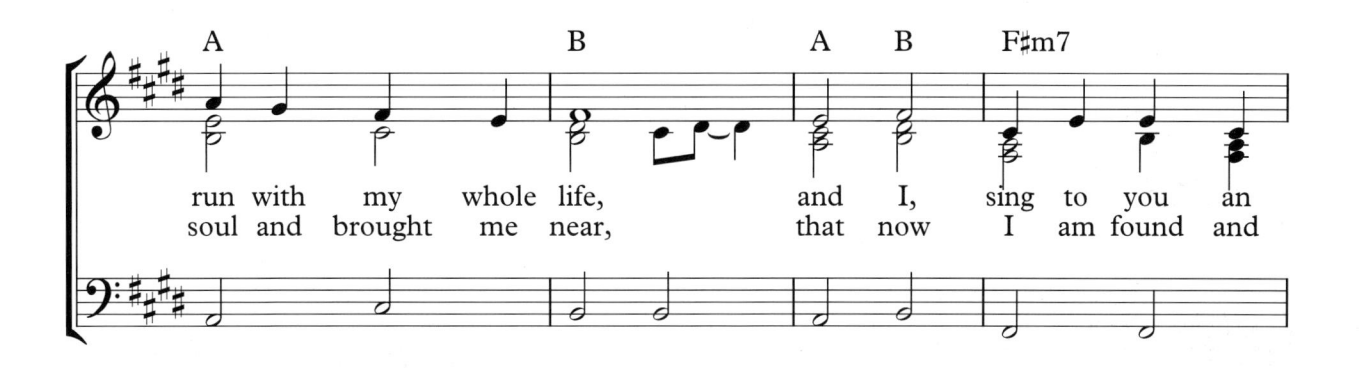

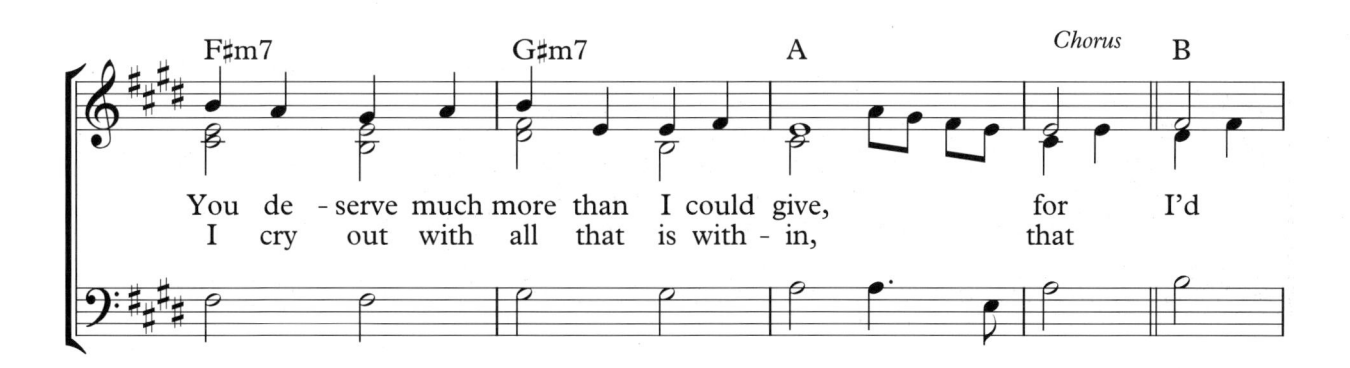

1. I know Your arms are o-pen wide, Father, in I run with my whole life, and I, sing to you an off-er-ing, the ve-ry best that I could bring, You de-serve much more than I could give, for I'd

2. It's like You whis-pered in my ear, when You saved my soul and brought me near, that now I am found and true it's You my heart a-dores, I am Yours, and I cry out with all that is with-in, that

Copyright © 1994 Kingsway's Thankyou Music, PO Box 75, Eastbourne, East Sussex, BN23 6NW, UK.
Used by permission.

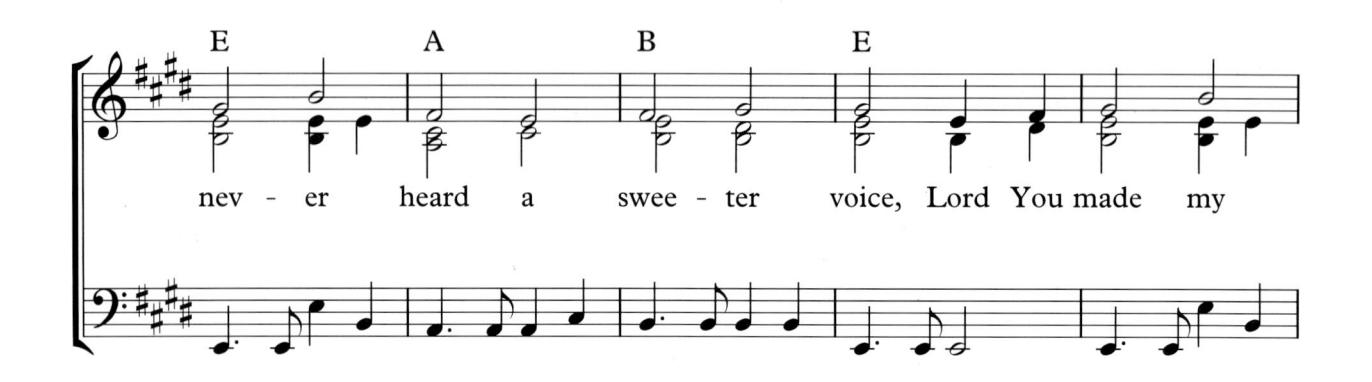

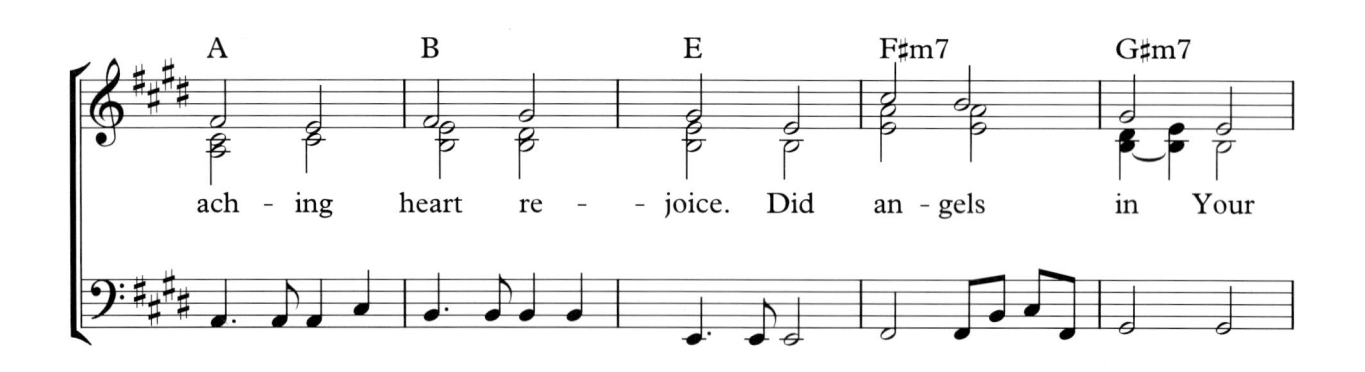

never heard a sweeter voice, Lord You made my aching heart rejoice. Did angels in Your presence sing, and all the courts of heaven ring.

Men: When You called my

Copyright © 1994 Kingsway's Thankyou Music, PO Box 75, Eastbourne, East Sussex, BN23 6NW, UK.
Used by permission.

Women: When You called my name.

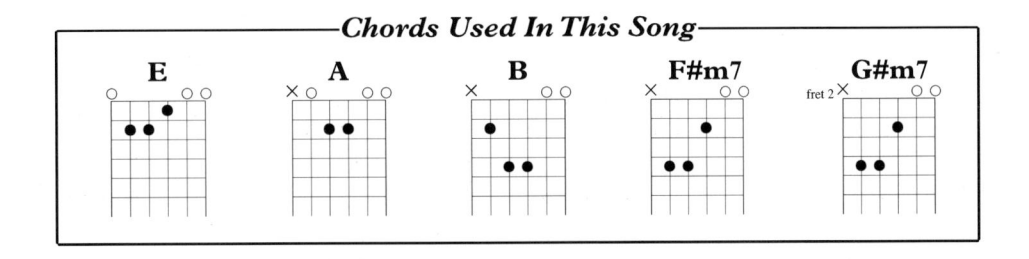

When You called my name.

When You called my name.

When You called my name.

Chords Used In This Song

E   A   B   F#m7   G#m7

Copyright © 1994 Kingsway's Thankyou Music, PO Box 75, Eastbourne, East Sussex, BN23 6NW, UK.
Used by permission.

16. I Remember The Day
Remember

Jeff Searles

1. I remember the day when You called my name,
when I lost my life to be found in You.
I remember the time when the world passed by
When I gladly gave it all up for You.

Chorus

Can You hear us, can You hear us we're lifting up the name of Jesus. He is the King of kings.

Verse

2. Know I love You Lord, for I know You love me. I know that You are always for me. E-ven though some-times,

Copyright © 1995 Big Bright Sky Music, 340 Patricia Drive, San Luis Obispo, Ca 93401, USA.
Used by permission.

I carry my shame. E-ven though some-times, I feel lost and not found. I know that You have called my name.

To chorus

Copyright © 1995 Big Bright Sky Music, 340 Patricia Drive, San Luis Obispo, Ca 93401, USA.
Used by permission.

17. It's Rising Up

Matt Redman & Martin Smith

Verse

1. It's rising up from coast to coast, from north to south, and east to west; the cry of hearts that love Your name, which with one voice we will proclaim.

The former things have taken place, can this be the new day of praise? A heav'nly song that comes to birth, and reaches out to all the earth. Oh,

Bridge

Copyright © 1995 Kingsway's Thankyou Music, PO Box 75, Eastbourne, East Sussex, BN23 6NW, UK.
Used by permission.

let the cry to nations ring, that all may come and all may sing:

Chorus
'Ho - ly is the Lord.'

'Ho - ly is the Lord.'

Verse
2. And we have heard the Lion's roar, that speaks of heaven's love and power. Is this the time, is

this the call that ushers in Your kingdom rule? Oh,
let the cry to nations ring, that all may come and all may sing:

Chorus
'Jesus is alive!'

'Jesus is a-

-live!"

Chords Used In This Song

E — C♯m7 — B — F♯m7 — G♯m7 — A — E

Verse — Chorus

Copyright © 1995 Kingsway's Thankyou Music, PO Box 75, Eastbourne, East Sussex, BN23 6NW, UK.
Used by permission.

18. I Was A Lost Soul
Turned Me Around

Matt Redman
Psalm 30
Malachi 4:2

Capo 2 (G)

1. I was a lost soul cap-tive to my his-tor-y. I stood a-shamed of things that had im-pris-oned me.
2. I live to thank the One who set me free from this, You took a hur-ting life and poured out ten-der-ness.

Copyright © 1995 Kingsway's Thankyou Music, PO Box 75, Eastbourne, East Sussex, BN23 6NW, UK.
Used by permission.

Bm7(Am7)　　　　**F♯m7(Em7)**

And then up from the grave, there rose
You brought me from the depths, and spared

D(C)　　　**E(D)**　　　**Bm7(Am7)**

— one like the sun, with heal-ing in Your wings,
— me from the pit, You clothed me with Your joy,

F♯m7(Em7)　**D(C)**　　　**E(D)**

You turned my life a-round.
and now my heart must sing.

Chorus

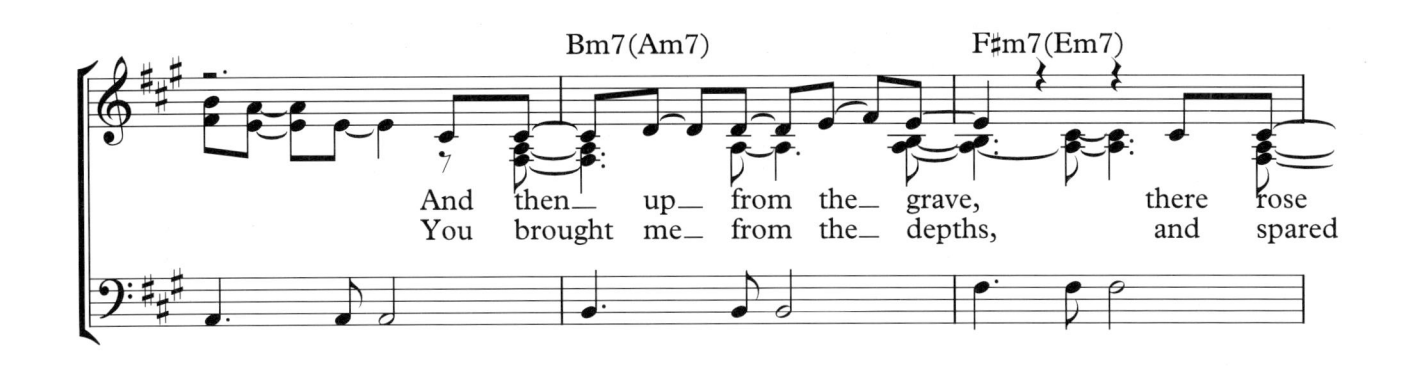

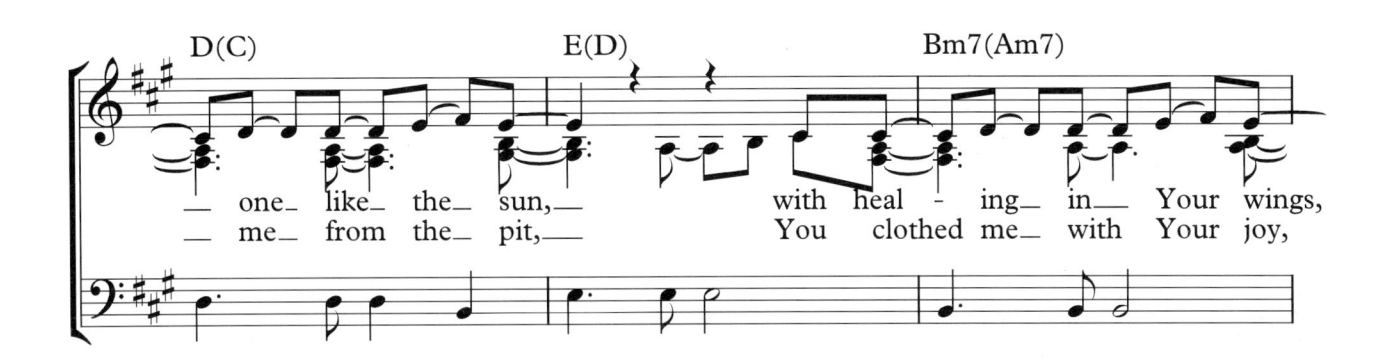

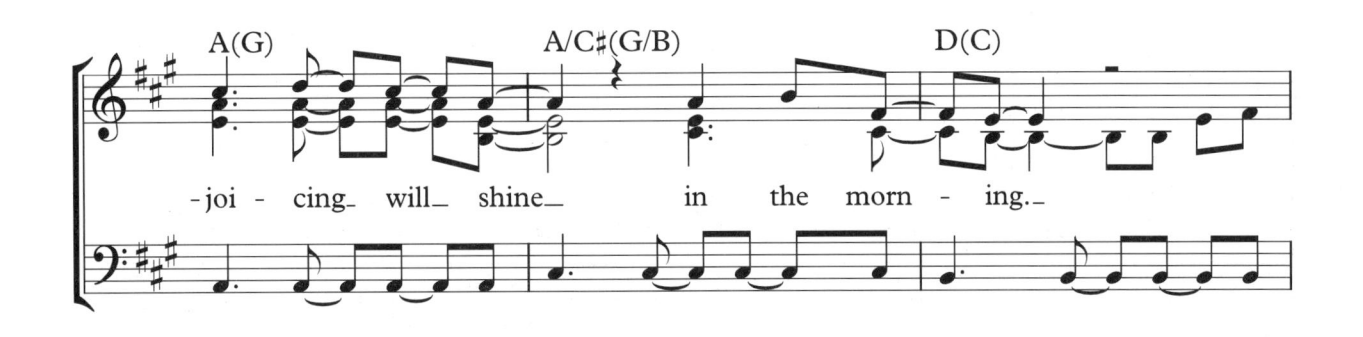

A(G)　　**A/C♯(G/B)**　　**D(C)**　　**E(D)**

Sor-row may come, hard-ship rain down, but re-

A(G)　　**A/C♯(G/B)**　　**D(C)**

-joi-cing will shine in the morn-ing.

Copyright © 1995 Kingsway's Thankyou Music, PO Box 75, Eastbourne, East Sussex, BN23 6NW, UK.
Used by permission.

You were there in the fast, You are here in the feast, gone is my shame, here is dancing.

1. You've turned me around.
2.

Bridge
I never thought I would see the light that I've seen;
You have brought love and grace and healing to me.

Copyright © 1995 Kingsway's Thankyou Music, PO Box 75, Eastbourne, East Sussex, BN23 6NW, UK.
Used by permission.

I ne-ver dreamt I could know the favour I've known,

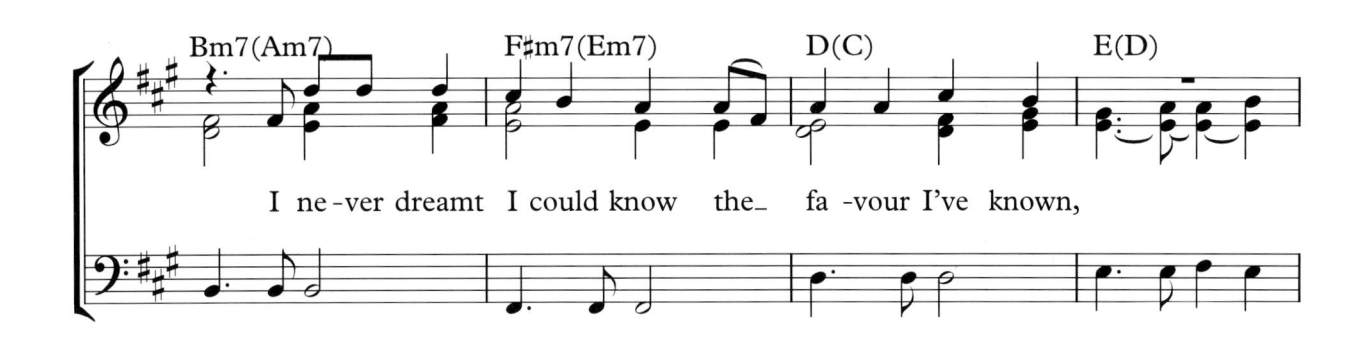

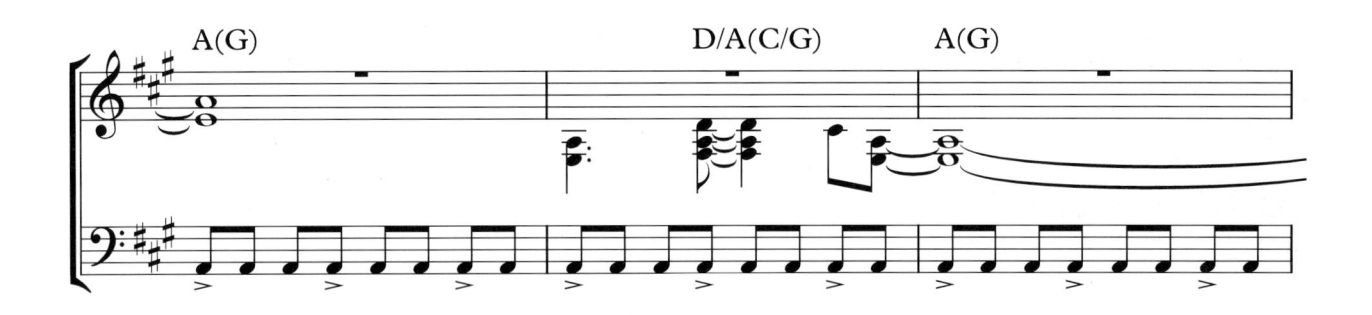

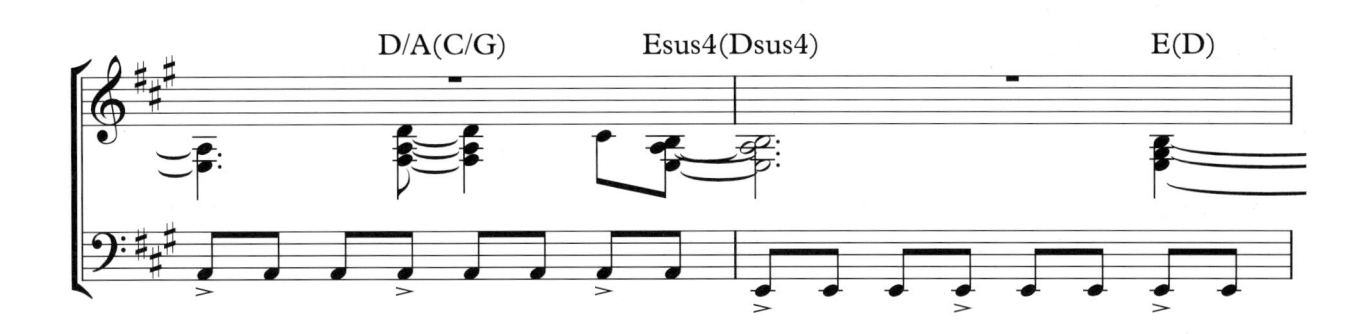

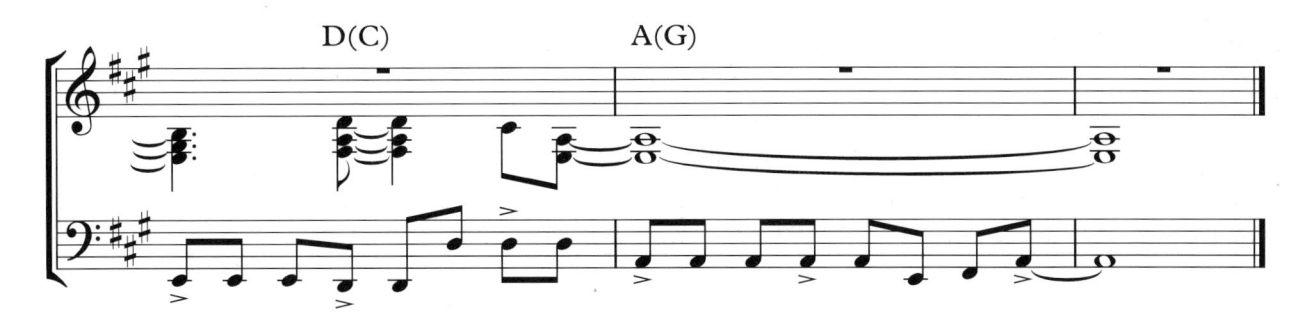

You heard my lonely cry and made me Your own.

Copyright © 1995 Kingsway's Thankyou Music, PO Box 75, Eastbourne, East Sussex, BN23 6NW, UK.
Used by permission.

19. I Will Offer Up My Life

Matt Redman

1. I will offer up my life in spirit and truth, pouring out the oil of love as my worship to You. In surrender I must give my ev'ry part; Lord, receive the sacri-

2. You deserve my every breath for You've paid the great cost; Giving up Your life to death, even death on a cross. You took all my shame away, there defeated my sin, Opened up the gates of

Copyright © 1994 Kingsway's Thankyou Music, PO Box 75, Eastbourne, East Sussex, BN23 6NW, UK.
Used by permission.

-fice of a bro-ken heart. Jesus, what can I give,
heav'n and have bec-koned me in.

what can I bring to so faith-ful a friend, to so lov-ing a King

Sav-iour, what can be said, what can be sung

as a praise of Your name for the things You have done?

Oh, my words could not tell, not ev-en in part, of the

Copyright © 1994 Kingsway's Thankyou Music, PO Box 75, Eastbourne, East Sussex, BN23 6NW, UK.
Used by permission.

debt of love that is owed by this thank-ful heart.

What can I give, what can I bring, what can I sing as an off-er-ing Lord?

Repeat as necessary

Chords Used In This Song

D　　G　　A7sus4　　Bm7　　Em7　　Dsus4/F♯

Copyright © 1994 Kingsway's Thankyou Music, PO Box 75, Eastbourne, East Sussex, BN23 6NW, UK.
Used by permission.

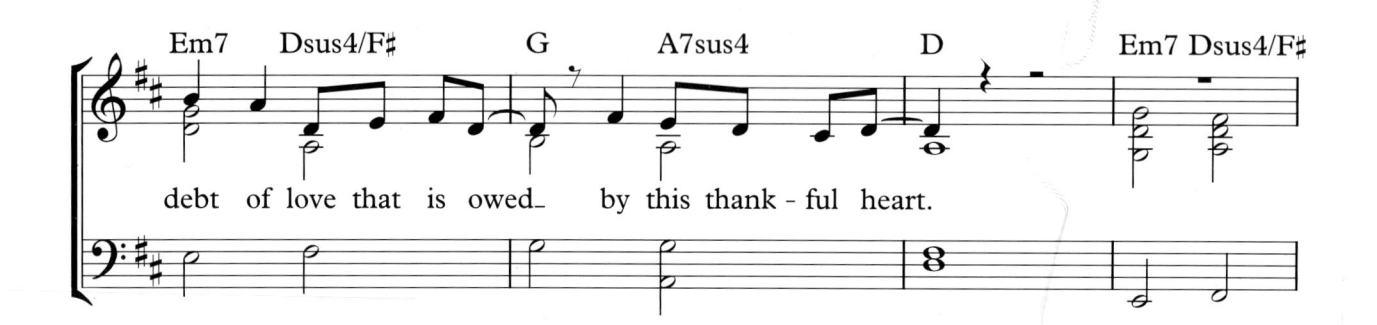

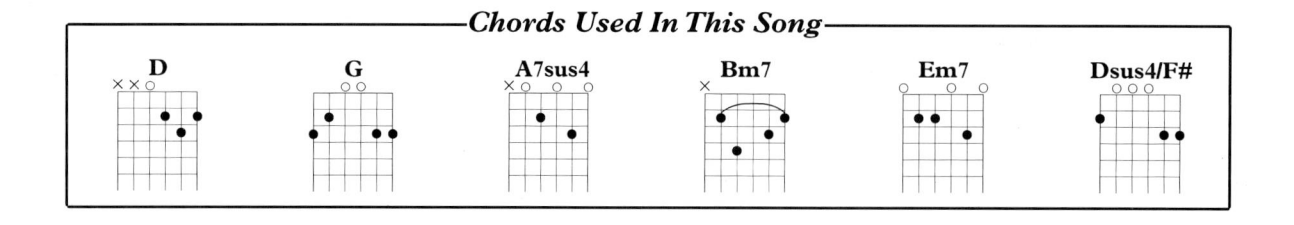

20. I Will Worship
You Are Worthy Of My Praise

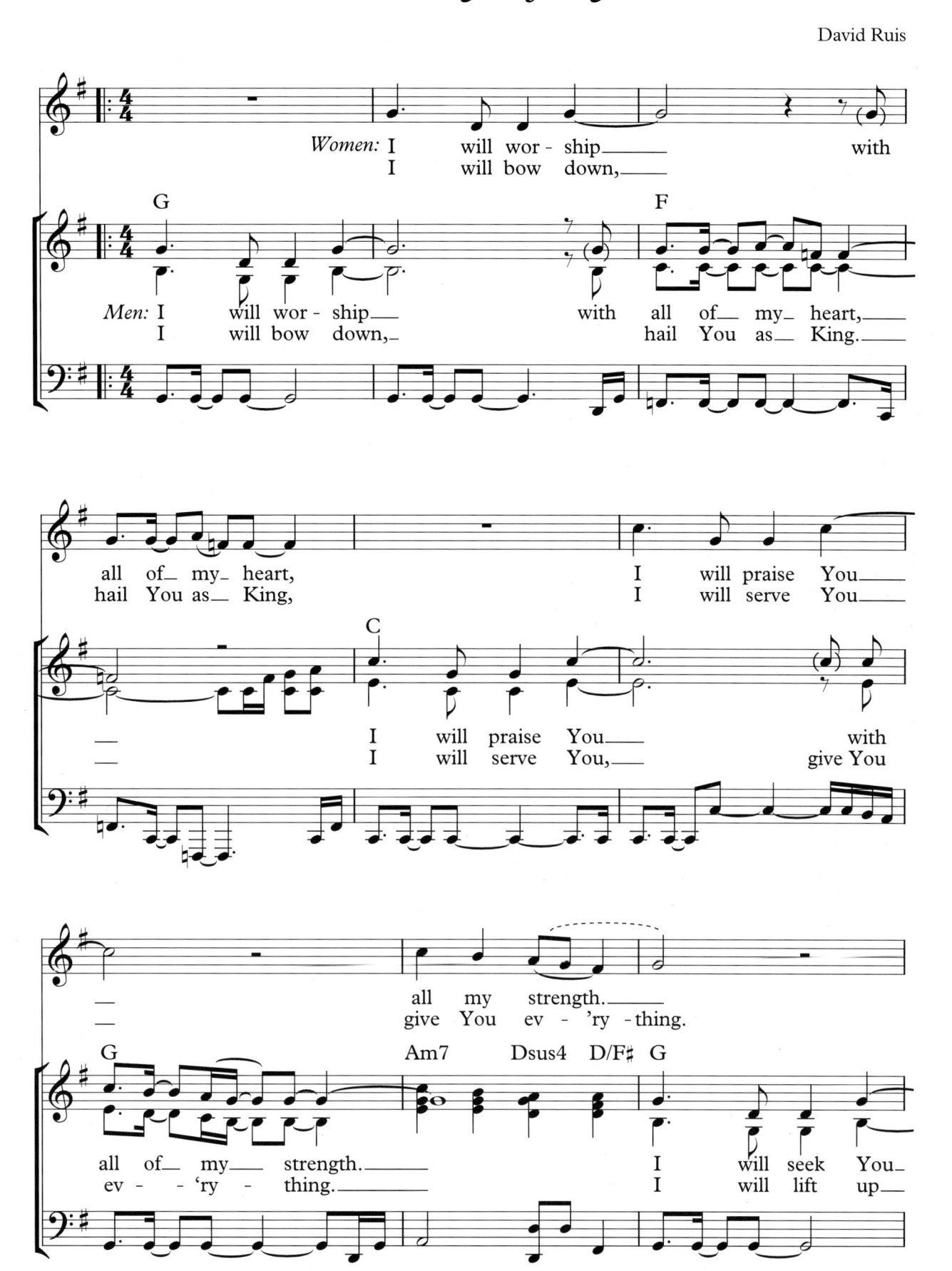

David Ruis

Women: I will worship with all of my heart,
I will bow down, hail You as King.

Men: I will worship with all of my heart,
I will bow down, hail You as King,

I will praise You with all of my strength.
I will serve You, give You ev-'ry-thing.

I will praise You with all of my strength.
I will serve You, give You ev-'ry-thing.

I will seek You
I will lift up

Copyright © 1993 Mercy Publishing/Kingsway's Thankyou Music, PO Box 75, Eastbourne, East Sussex, BN23 6NW, UK.
Used by permission.

Copyright © 1993 Mercy Publishing/Kingsway's Thankyou Music, PO Box 75, Eastbourne, East Sussex, BN23 6NW, UK.
Used by permission.

all my worship, I will give You all my praise.

You alone I long to worship, You alone are worthy of my praise.

Copyright © 1993 Mercy Publishing/Kingsway's Thankyou Music, PO Box 75, Eastbourne, East Sussex, BN23 6NW, UK.
Used by permission.

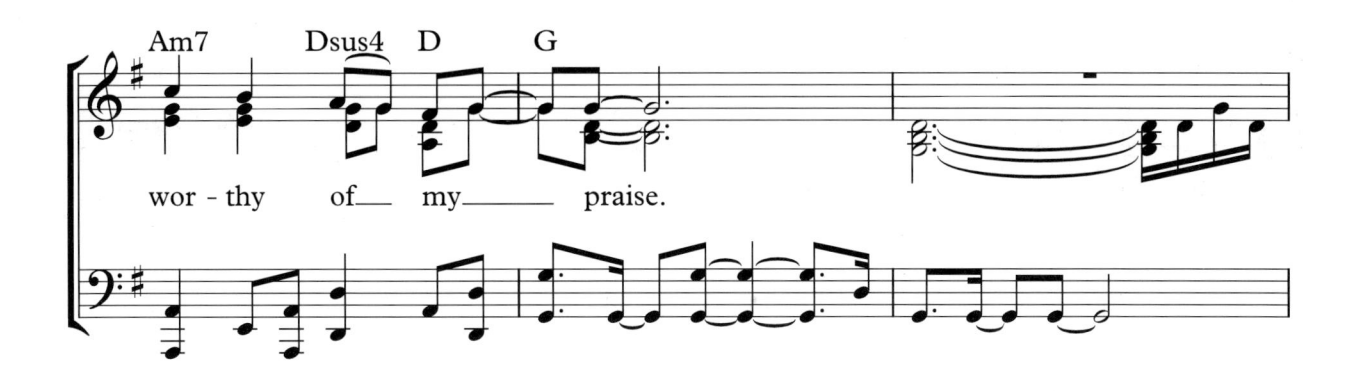

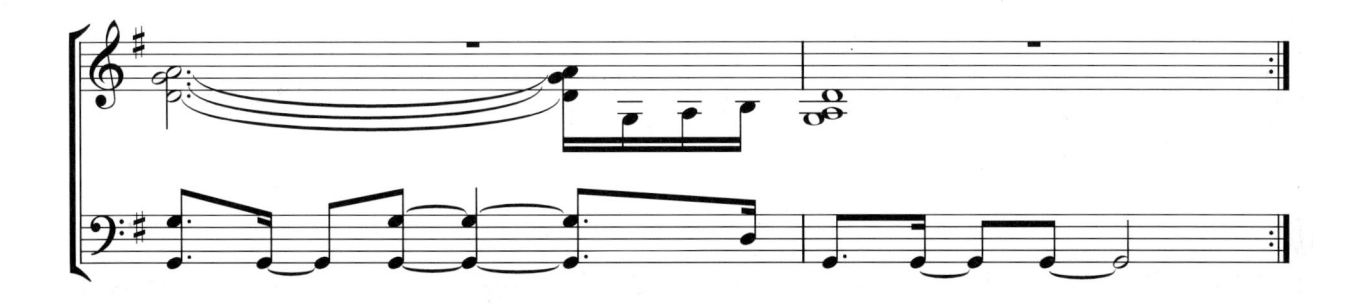

21. Jesus, Is This Song of Love

Matt Redman

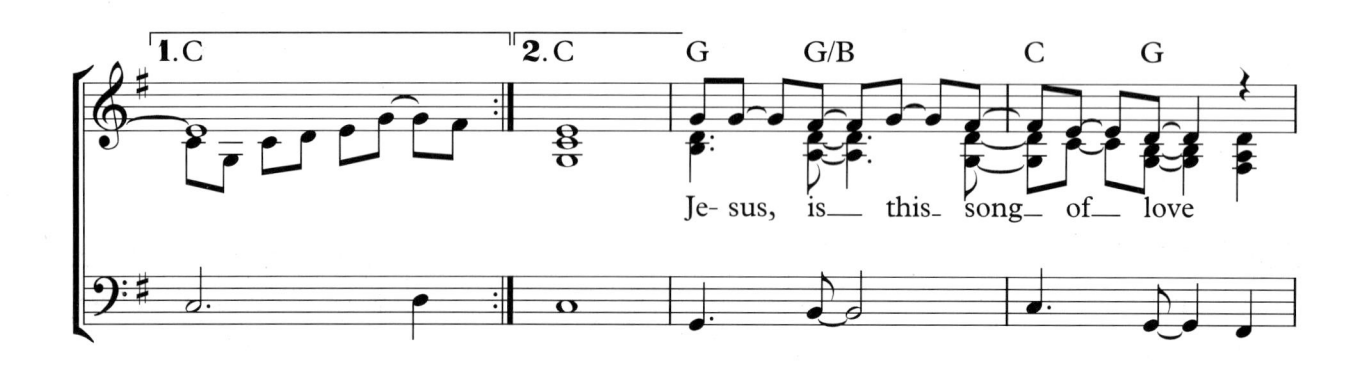

Jesus, is this song of love heard up in the heav'ns above? Though I stumble and I stray, turn to me again.

Copyright © 1995 Kingsway's Thankyou Music, PO Box 75, Eastbourne, East Sussex, BN23 6NW, UK.
Used by permission.

Do not look upon my sin, but, dear Lord, look deep within; see the fire that burns therein — passion for Your name. For even though You are a King, I hear You call me as Your friend; is this a love that knows no bounds and beckons even me? And though Your name is great

Copyright © 1995 Kingsway's Thankyou Music, PO Box 75, Eastbourne, East Sussex, BN23 6NW, UK.
Used by permission.

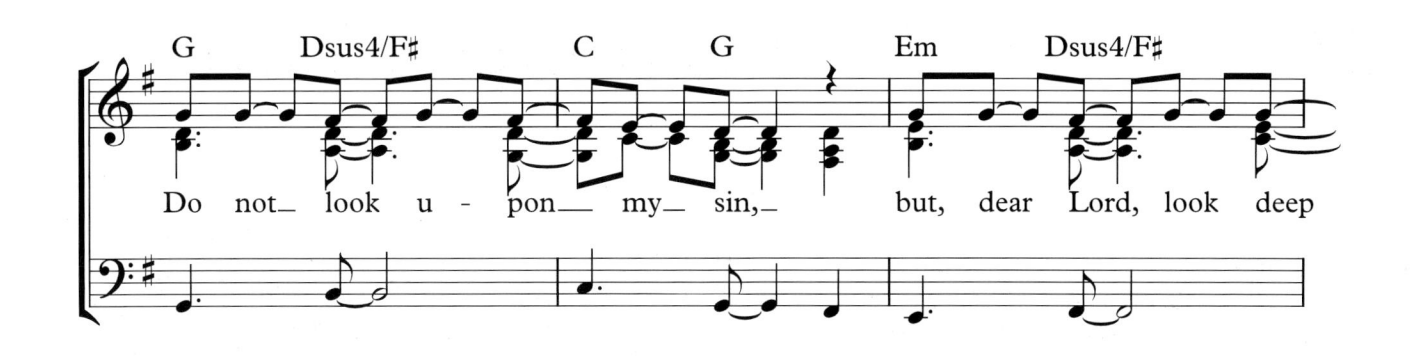

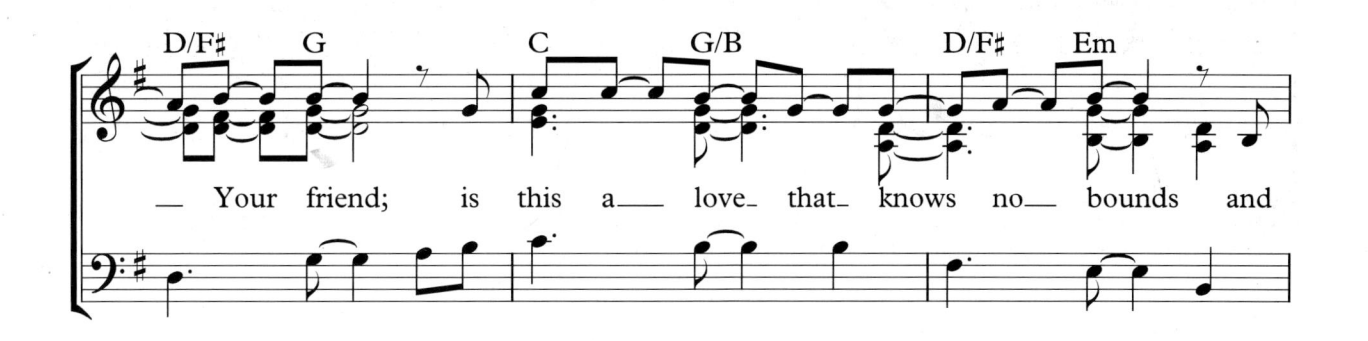

-ly feared, You still would draw a sinner near. Turn and with a gracious ear, hear my song of love.

Chords Used In This Song

Em   Dsus4/F#   G   C   G/B   D   D/F#

Copyright © 1995 Kingsway's Thankyou Music, PO Box 75, Eastbourne, East Sussex, BN23 6NW, UK.
Used by permission.

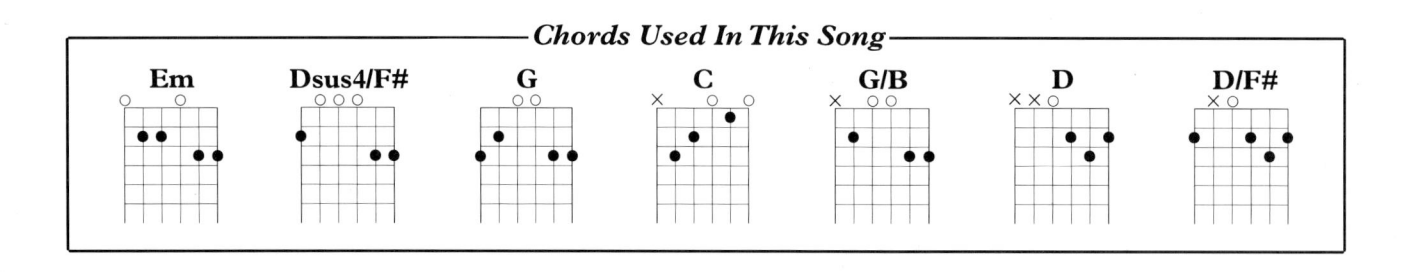

Consider therefore the kindness and sternness of God.

Romans 11: 22.

22. Let Your Fire Burn In Me

Fabienne Pons
Translation: Judith Robertson

Chorus

Let Your fi - re burn in me.
Let Your fi - re burn in me.

Burn - ing with love, O let me be.
Burn - ing with joy, O let me be.

Verse

1. Be - fore Your face as sweet per - fume, my prayer will rise.
2. In - to Your pre - sence my heart calls and so I come.
3. I come to wor - ship, to a - dore, to con - tem - plate.

And I will lift my hands to You in li - ving sac - ri - fice.
For You are migh - ty and I bow be - fore Your ho - ly throne.
This li - ving tem - ple, to my Lord I come to con - se - crate.

Copyright © 1982 Fabienne Pons/LTC, 92 rue Rebeval, 75019 Paris, France.
Used by permission.

23. My Jesus I Love Thee

R. Featherstone & A. Gordon

Capo 3 (D)

1. My Jesus I love thee, I know thou art mine. For thee, all the follies of sin I resign. My gracious Redeemer, my Saviour art thou, If ever I loved thee, my Jesus 'tis now.

2. I love thee because thou has first loved me. And purchased my pardon on Calvary's tree. I love thee for ever a-dore thee in heaven so bright. I'll sing with the wearing the thorns on thy brow. If ever I loved thee, my Jesus 'tis now.

3. In mansions of glory an endless delight. I'll ever adore thee in heaven so bright. I'll sing with the glittering crown on my brow. If ever I loved thee, my Jesus 'tis now.

24. Rags To Riches

Matt Redman
Phillipians 3: 7, Romans 9: 23
Matthew 6: 21, Jeremiah 9: 23, 24

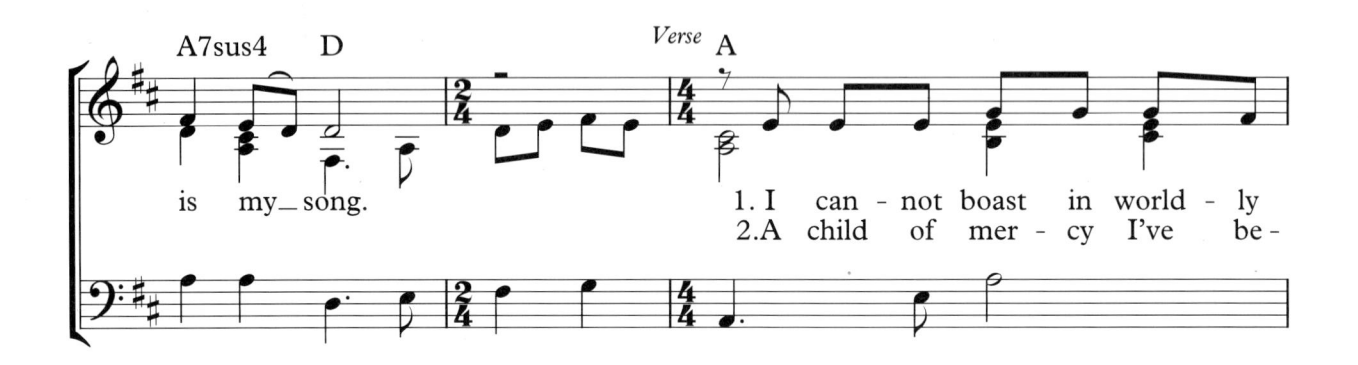

Chorus

Rags to rich-es is my song, I had no-thing in this world; but You filled my emp-ty cup, and You healed my way-ward soul. Rags to rich-es is my song.

Verse

1. I can-not boast in world-ly gain; like dust to dust it will soon fade a-way.
2. A child of mer-cy I've be-come You've rich in love, and I was so poor.

Copyright © 1995 Kingsway's Thankyou Music, PO Box 75, Eastbourne, East Sussex, BN23 6NW, UK.
Used by permission.

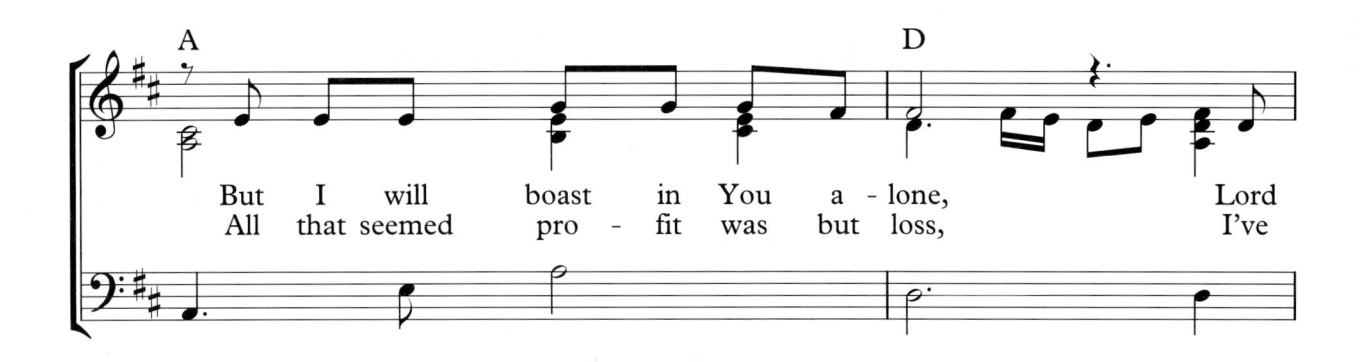

But I will boast in You a-lone, Lord Jesus Christ, my wealth, my all.

All that seemed pro-fit was but loss, I've tra-ded all for this pearl of price.

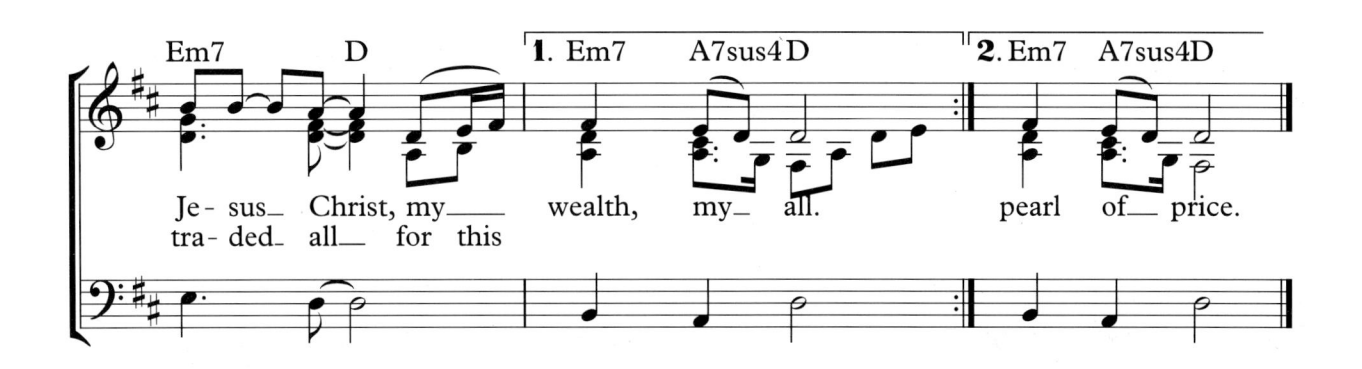

Chords Used In This Song

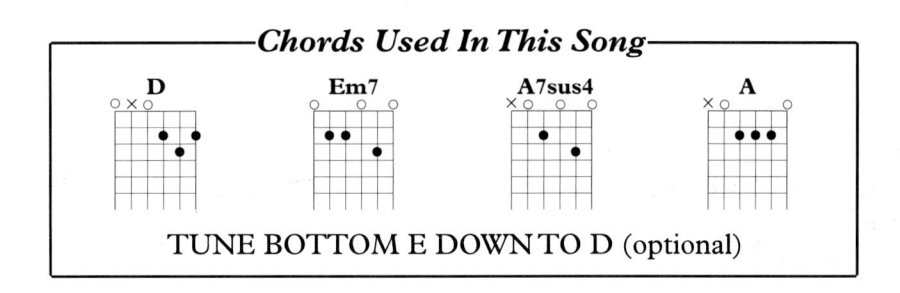

D   Em7   A7sus4   A

TUNE BOTTOM E DOWN TO D (optional)

Copyright © 1995 Kingsway's Thankyou Music, PO Box 75, Eastbourne, East Sussex, BN23 6NW, UK.
Used by permission.

25. Shout To The Lord

Judith Robertson

Chorus

Shout to the Lord all You peoples and speak out the wonders of His name. Honour your Lord giving Him praises all His wonders proclaim

Verse

1. You are Lord! (You are Lord!) Mighty in Your deeds! (Mighty in Your deeds!)
2. You are King! (You are King!) Awesome is Your power! (Awesome is Your power!)
3. Mighty God! (Mighty God!) Setting captives free! (Setting captives free!)
4. Songs of praise! (Songs of praise!) Break out in our hearts! (Break out in our hearts!)

We honour You giving You praises. You are worthy, O Lord.

Copyright © 1989 Judith Robertson/LTC, 92 rue Rebeval, 75019 Paris, France.
Used by permission.

Come let us sing for joy to the Lord;
Let us shout aloud
To the rock of our salvation.
Let us come before Him with thanksgiving
And exalt Him with music and song.

Psalm 95: 1,2.

26. Shout To The Lord
For He Is Worthy

Elizabeth Bourbouze
Translation: Judith Robertson

Chorus

Shout to the Lord "Yes!" Ce - le - brate!

For He is wor - thy of our prai - ses.

Shout to the Lord "Yes!" You are great!

And You are wor - thy of our prai - ses.

Verse

1. God has said: "I'll de - li - ver them."
2. God has said: "I will ov - er come."
3. God has said: "I will send them out."

Copyright © 1994 Elizabeth Bourbouze/LTC, 92 rue Rebeval, 75019 Paris, France.
Used by permission.

He has kept His word, giving us salvation.
All His enemies have been crushed and thrown down.
He has chosen us to say to the whole world,

For our God is good, and we are forgiven.
For our God is great. In the heavens He is Lord.
Holy is our God, serve the Father in His Light.

For our God is good, healing us with compassion.
For our God is great. He accomplishes His Word.
Holy is our God, live for Him and be upright.

He is good.
He is great.
Holy Lord.

Copyright © 1994 Elizabeth Bourbouze/LTC, 92 rue Rebeval, 75019 Paris, France.
Used by permission.

27. Sing A Song Of Celebration
We Will Dance

David Ruis

Sing a song of celebration, lift up a shout of praise, for the Bridegroom will come, the glorious one, and oh, we will look on his face, We'll go to a

Dance with all your might, lift up your hands and clap for joy. The time's drawing near when he will appear, And oh, we will stand by his side, a strong,

Copyright © 1993 Mercy Publishing/Kingsway's Thankyou Music, PO Box 75, Eastbourne, East Sussex, BN23 6NW, UK.
Used by permission.

1. much better place.

2. pure, spotless bride.

Chorus
Oh, we will dance on the streets that are golden, the glorious bride and the great Son of Man. From ev'ry tongue and tribe and nation will join in the song of the Lamb.

Copyright © 1993 Mercy Publishing/Kingsway's Thankyou Music, PO Box 75, Eastbourne, East Sussex, BN23 6NW, UK.
Used by permission.

Men: Sing a-loud for the time of re-joic-ing is near.

Women: Sing a-loud for the time of re-joic-ing is near.

Men: near. The ris-en King, our groom, is soon to ap-pear.

soon to ap-pear. The wed-ding

The wed-ding feast to come is now near at hand.

Copyright © 1993 Mercy Publishing/Kingsway's Thankyou Music, PO Box 75, Eastbourne, East Sussex, BN23 6NW, UK.
Used by permission.

feast to come is now near at hand.

Dsus4   D   Dsus2   D   Dsus4   D

Lift up your voice, pro-claim the

Lift up your voice, pro-claim the com-ing

Dsus2   D   Dsus4   D   Dsus2

com - ing Lamb.

To chorus

Lamb.

D   Dsus4   D   Dsus2

Copyright © 1993 Mercy Publishing/Kingsway's Thankyou Music, PO Box 75, Eastbourne, East Sussex, BN23 6NW, UK.
Used by permission.

28. The Cross Has Said It All

Matt Redman and Martin Smith
Psalm 103: 11,12
Ephesians 3: 18

Capo 2 (G)

Intro

[Musical notation with chords: A(G) D(C) A(G) E(D) A(G) D(C) A(G) E(D) A(G) D(C) A(G) E(D) A(G) D(C) A(G) E(D) A(G)]

Verse

The cross has said it all,
cross has said it all,

— the cross has said it all. I
— the cross has said it all. I

can't de-ny what You have shown, the cross speaks of a God
ne-ver re-cog-nised Your touch, un-til I met You at

Copyright © 1995 Kingsway's Thankyou Music, PO Box 75, Eastbourne, East Sussex, BN23 6NW, UK.
Used by permission.

_ of_ love; there dis-played_ for_ all_ to_ see,
_ the_ cross. We are fal--len,_ dust_ to_ dust,

Je- sus Christ, our_ on-ly_ hope a mess-age of_ the_ Fa-
how could You do_ this_ for_ us?_ Son of God_ shed_ pre-

-ther's heart, "Come, my child-ren, come_ on_ home."
-cious blood, who can comp-re-hend_ this_ love?

Chorus

As high as the heav'ns are a-bove_ the_ earth, so

high is the mea-sure of_ Your_ great love, as far as the east is_ from

Copyright © 1995 Kingsway's Thankyou Music, PO Box 75, Eastbourne, East Sussex, BN23 6NW, UK.
Used by permission.

Lyrics:
— from west, so far have You taken our sins from us. As from us. 2. The from us.

Bridge
How high, how wide, how deep. How high, how wide, how deep.

How high, how wide, how deep. How high, how wide, how deep.

How high!

Copyright © 1995 Kingsway's Thankyou Music, PO Box 75, Eastbourne, East Sussex, BN23 6NW, UK.
Used by permission.

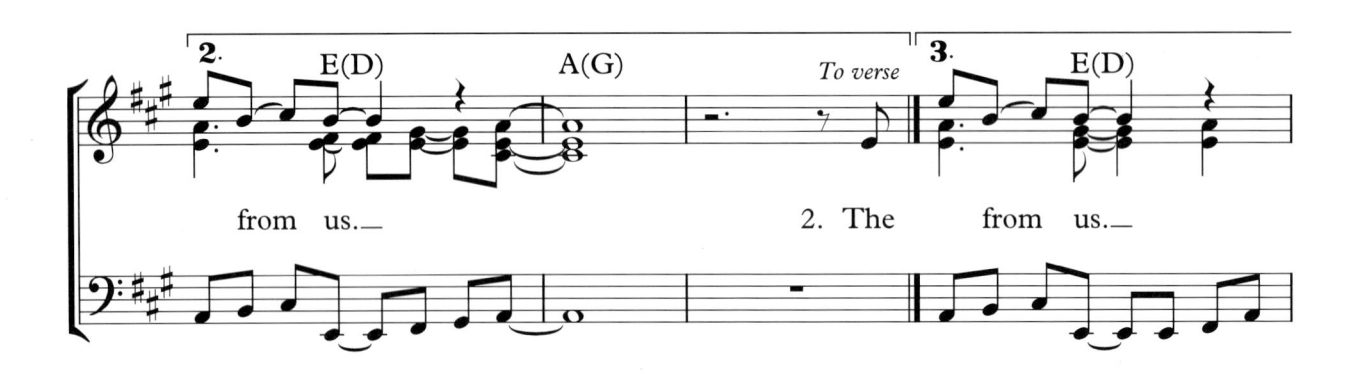

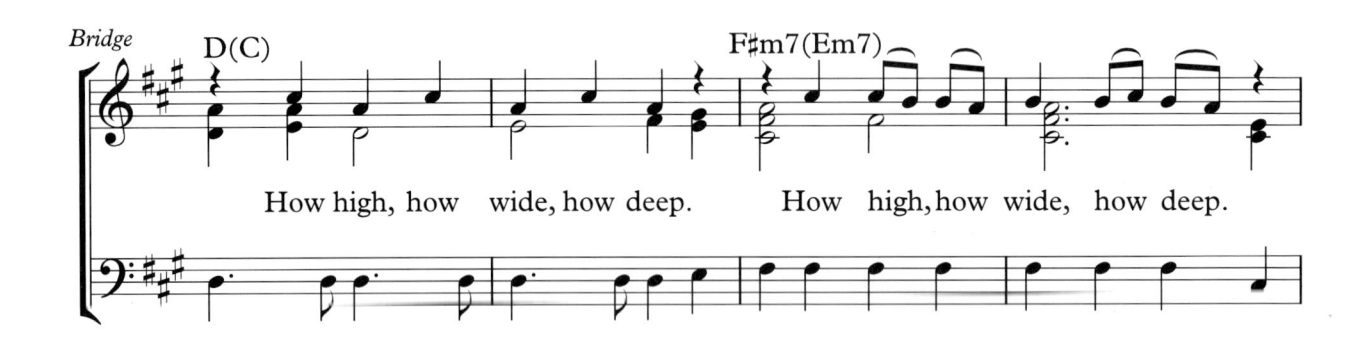

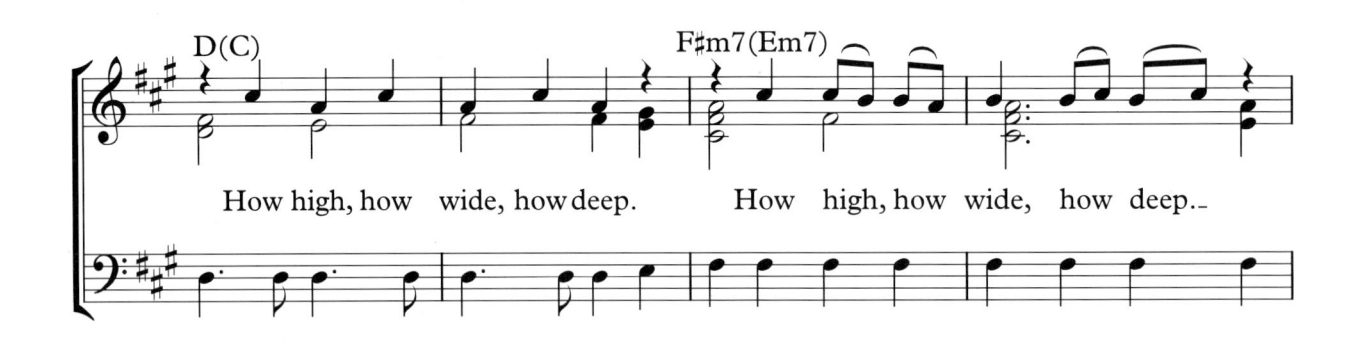

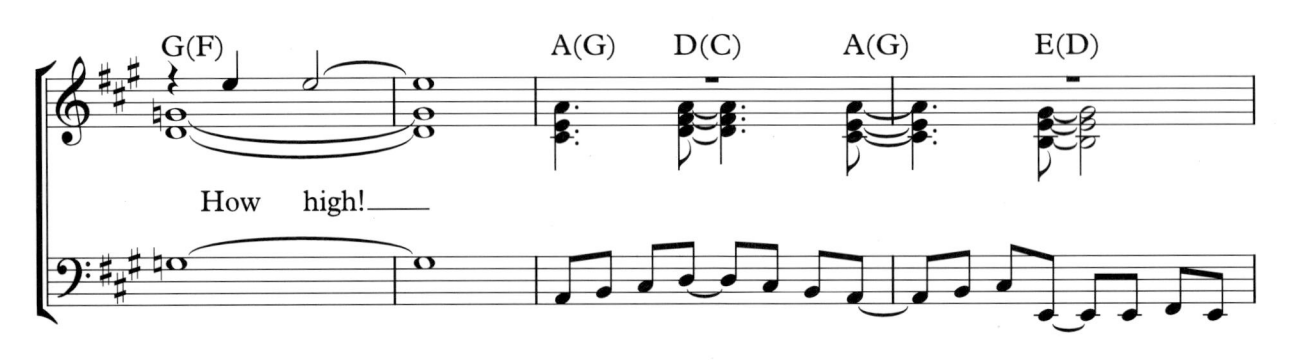

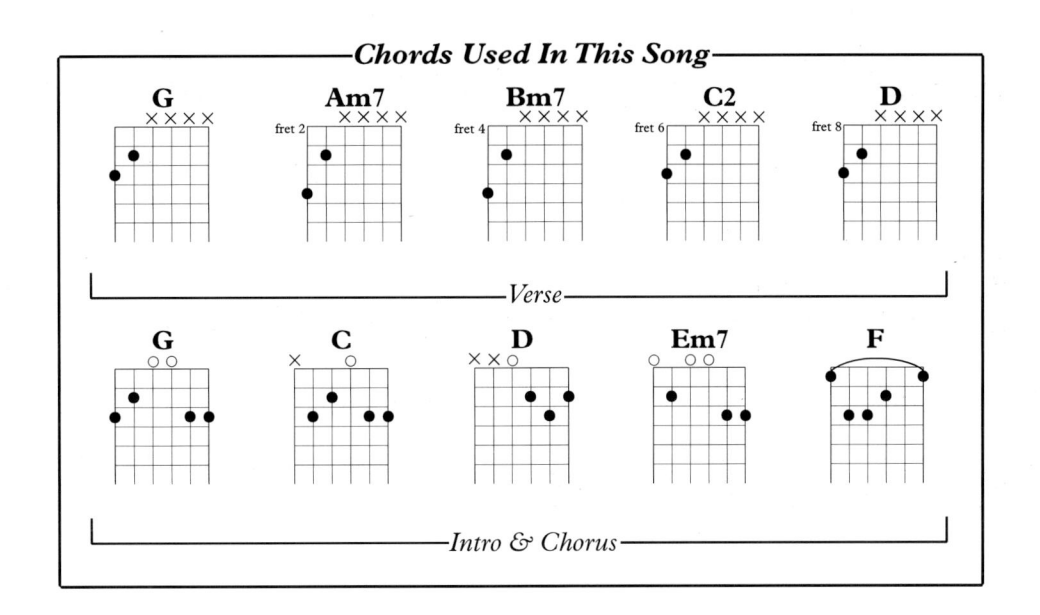

Chords Used In This Song

Verse: G, Am7, Bm7, C2, D

Intro & Chorus: G, C, D, Em7, F

Copyright © 1995 Kingsway's Thankyou Music, PO Box 75, Eastbourne, East Sussex, BN23 6NW, UK.
Used by permission.

29. They That Wait On The Lord

Kevin Prosch

Chorus 1

They that wait on the Lord will re-new their strength. Run and not be wea-ry, walk and not fai-nt.

(1st time: They that wait)

Verse

Do you not know, have you not heard, my Fa-ther does not grow wea-ry, He'll give pas-sion to a will-ing heart, ev-

Copyright © 1993 7th Time Music/Kingsway's Thankyou Music, PO Box 75, Eastbourne, East Sussex, BN23 6NW, UK.
Used by permission.

Chorus 2

-en the youths get tired and faint, but strength will come for those who wait. They that wait on the Lord will renew their strength. Run and not grow weary, walk and not faint.

(1st time: They that wait)

Ending

who wait. I will wait, I will wait, I will wait on You. I will run
I will run, I will run with You. I will run
My love, My love, My love for You. My love

Copyright © 1993 7th Time Music/Kingsway's Thankyou Music, PO Box 75, Eastbourne, East Sussex, BN23 6NW, UK.
Used by permission.

30. This Means I Love You

Matt Redman

Chorus

This means I love You, singing this song, Lord I don't have the words, but I do have the will. And this means I love You, that I take up my cross, I will sing as I walk out this love.

Copyright © 1995 Kingsway's Thankyou Music, PO Box 75, Eastbourne, East Sussex, BN23 6NW, UK.
Used by permission.

Verse

1. Jesus, this life is for You, every-thing, Lord that I do; these are the deeds that are pleasing and ways that are pure, Lord, may my life bear this fruit.

2. For these are the plans of my heart, yet often I'm missing the mark. see my desire to live in Your truth this surely means I love You.

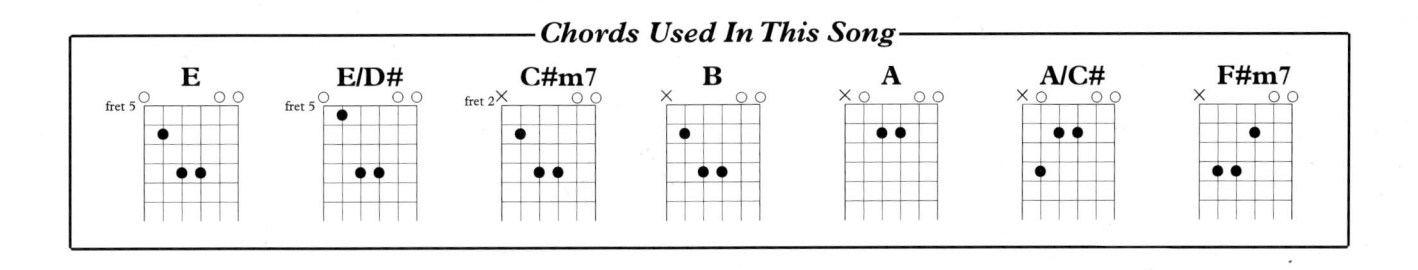

To chorus.

Chords Used In This Song

E   E/D#   C#m7   B   A   A/C#   F#m7

Copyright © 1995 Kingsway's Thankyou Music, PO Box 75, Eastbourne, East Sussex, BN23 6NW, UK.
Used by permission.

31. Wash Me And Make Me Yours
Gloria

Jeff Searles

1. Wash me and make me Yours for You have won Your prize. I place my sin on the cross, oh Lord, because of my crime. Eternal fire burn in me Holy God, I embrace Your life, You have won my heart.

Copyright © 1995 Big Bright Sky Music, 340 Patricia Drive, San Luis Obispo, Ca 93401, USA.
Used by permission.

Chorus lyrics: Glo-ri-a, Glo-ri-a, Glo-ri-a. (x3, 2nd time to bridge)

Verse 2: I will break open my life like the sweet perfume and this song will rise up to You. For You have shown Your heart and I will

Copyright © 1995 Big Bright Sky Music, 340 Patricia Drive, San Luis Obispo, Ca 93401, USA.
Used by permission.

never be the same. I will pour out my love on to You as an offering of praise. I will never look back.

Bridge
I will follow You and You will own my heart. I will follow You and You

Copyright © 1995 Big Bright Sky Music, 340 Patricia Drive, San Luis Obispo, Ca 93401, USA.
Used by permission.

will own my heart. I'll never look back.

Ending

You who knew no sin stepped down from heaven in Him, You have won my heart.

Copyright © 1995 Big Bright Sky Music, 340 Patricia Drive, San Luis Obispo, Ca 93401, USA.
Used by permission.

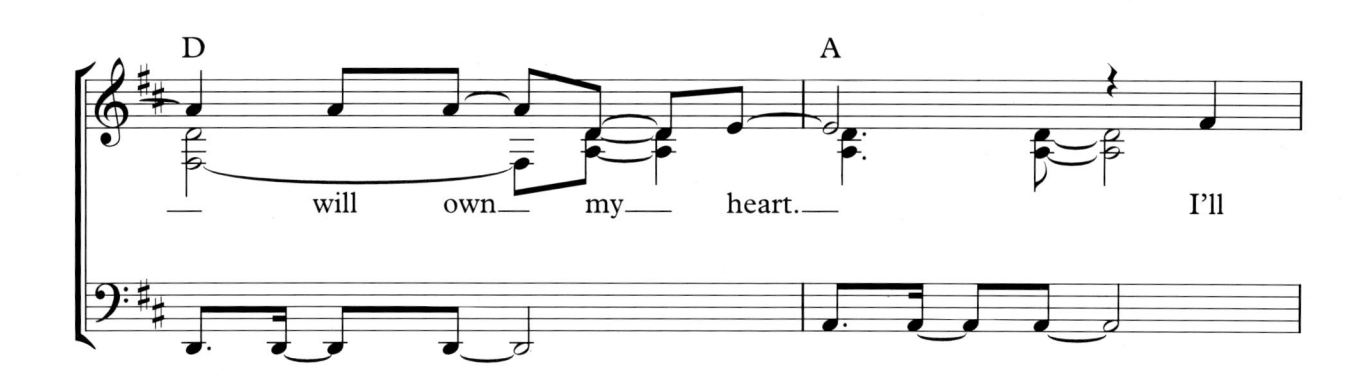

32. Well, I Hear They're Singing
I've Found Jesus

Martin Smith

1. Well I hear they're singing in the streets that Jesus is alive, and all creation shouts aloud that Jesus is alive. Now surely we can all be changed 'cos Jesus is alive, and

   feel like dancing in the streets 'cos Jesus is alive, to join with all who celebrate that Jesus is alive. Well the joy of God is in this town 'cos Jesus is alive, for

Copyright © 1994 Curious? Music U.K./Kingsway's Thankyou Music, PO Box 75, Eastbourne, East Sussex, BN23 6NW, UK.
Used by permission.

ev'ry-bo-dy here can know that Jesus is a-live. And
ev'ry-bo-dy's seen the truth that Jesus is a-live.

I will live for all my days, to raise a ban-ner of truth and light.

To sing a-bout my Sa-viour's love. And the

best thing that hap-pened it was the day I met You.
I've found

Copyright © 1994 Curious? Music U.K./Kingsway's Thankyou Music, PO Box 75, Eastbourne, East Sussex, BN23 6NW, UK.
Used by permission.

Je-sus. I've found Je-sus. I've found Je-sus. I've found Je-sus.

Last time to ending.

1. A 2. Well I
2. A *Bridge* Well You

lift-ed me from where I was, set my feet u-pon a rock,

Copyright © 1994 Curious? Music U.K./Kingsway's Thankyou Music, PO Box 75, Eastbourne, East Sussex, BN23 6NW, UK.
Used by permission.

humbled that You even knew about me. Now I have chosen to believe, believing that You've chosen me, I was lost but now I've found: I've found

To chorus, then to ending

Ending

Jesus.

Chords Used In This Song

Verse: E, A, C#m7, B
Chorus: E, A, F#m11

The music for Martin Smith's other songs can be obtained by telephoning: 01903 733031

Copyright © 1994 Curious? Music U.K./Kingsway's Thankyou Music, PO Box 75, Eastbourne, East Sussex, BN23 6NW, UK.
Used by permission.

33. We've Had A Light
Surely The Time Has Come

Capo 2 (A)

Matt Redman

Verse

We've had a light shine in our midst, we've felt Your pre-sence, we've known Your peace, and though this bless-ing comes to us free it car-ries a cha-llenge to go. We've had a feast laid on for us, You have com-manded "Bring in the lost", there's food for all, an-y who'd come, an-y who would know Your Son. We

Copyright © 1995 Kingsway's Thankyou Music, PO Box 75, Eastbourne, East Sussex, BN23 6NW, UK.
Used by permission.

know it's time to go, we've heard the cries of all of the earth.

Send us with power, we can-not do it a-lone. With

pas-sion for the lost we'll take the truth,

what-ev'r the cost; time is so short,

we can-not squan-der this love. Sur-ely the

time has come,

Copyright © 1995 Kingsway's Thankyou Music, PO Box 75, Eastbourne, East Sussex, BN23 6NW, UK.
Used by permission.

Copyright © 1995 Kingsway's Thankyou Music, PO Box 75, Eastbourne, East Sussex, BN23 6NW, UK.
Used by permission.

34. When Your Spirit And Your Fire
Come, Fire Of God

Fabienne Pons
Translation: Judith Robertson

1. When Your Spirit and Your fire fill my life with cleansing power, my soul and my heart cry "Lord, come!" When Your Spirit and Your fire fill me with transforming power, my soul and my heart cry: "Lord, come!"

2. When Your Spirit and Your fire fill me with renewing power, my soul and my heart cry "Lord, come!" When Your Spirit and Your fire fill me with consuming power, my soul and my heart cry: "Lord, come!"

2nd time to chorus 2

Copyright © 1991 Fabienne Pons/LTC, 92 rue Rebeval, 75019 Paris, France.
Used by permission.

Chorus 1

Dm | **B♭maj7**
Burn, fire of God. Burn, fire of God.

E♭ | **Asus4**
Come, refining flame, set my life ablaze.

Dm | **B♭maj7**
Burn, fire of God. Burn, fire of God.

E♭
seal me with this word: "Ho-

Asus4 | **A** | **Asus4** | **A** *To verse 2*
-liness to the Lord."

Copyright © 1991 Fabienne Pons/LTC, 92 rue Rebeval, 75019 Paris, France.
Used by permission.

Chorus 2

Burn, fire of God. Burn, fire of God. wake my sleeping heart and set my soul alight. Burn, fire of God. Burn, fire of God. Burn, consume and fill with Your love and Your zeal.

Copyright © 1991 Fabienne Pons/LTC, 92 rue Rebeval, 75019 Paris, France.
Used by permission.

35. When You've Been Broken
Kiss The Son

Kevin Prosch

Verse

1. When you've been broken, broken to pieces.

And Your heart begins to faint 'cause you don't understand. And when there is nothing to rake from the ashes. And you can't even walk on — to the fields of praise.

Copyright © 1994 7th Time Music/Kingsway's Thankyou Music, PO Box 75, Eastbourne, East Sussex, BN23 6NW, UK.
Used by permission.

G ... *Chorus* **G/F♯**

But I ___ bow down

C2 ... **Dsus4**

and kiss the Son. ___

D ... **G/F♯**

Oh, ___ and I ___ bow down

E2 ... **Dsus4** ... **D**

and kiss the Son. ___ Let the

G

praise of the Lord be ___ in my mouth. Let the

D ... **G**

praise of the Lord be ___ in my mouth. ___ Well, though You slay me,

Copyright © 1994 7th Time Music/Kingsway's Thankyou Music, PO Box 75, Eastbourne, East Sussex, BN23 6NW, UK.
Used by permission.

I will trust You, Lord. Well, though You slay me,

I will trust You, Lord. Though You slay me,

I will trust You, Lord.

Last time to ending

Though You slay me, I will trust You, Lord.

Verse

2. When the rock falls, falls u-pon you.

And you get ground to dust

Copyright © 1994 7th Time Music/Kingsway's Thankyou Music, PO Box 75, Eastbourne, East Sussex, BN23 6NW, UK.
Used by permission.

no mu-sic for your pain. You o-pen the win-dows, the win-dows of heaven. And then You o-pened me and You crushed me like a rose. But I

Ending

Copyright © 1994 7th Time Music/Kingsway's Thankyou Music, PO Box 75, Eastbourne, East Sussex, BN23 6NW, UK.
Used by permission.

ACETATE MASTERS

The following pages are master copies to make acetate sheets for overhead projection.

Can I ascend the hill of the Lord?
Can I stand in that holy place?
There to approach the glory of my God;
Come towards to seek Your face.
Purify my heart and purify my hands,
For I know it is
On holy ground I'll stand.

Chorus:
I'm coming up the mountain, Lord;
I'm seeking You and You alone.
I know that I will be transformed,
My heart unveiled before You.
I'm longing for Your presence, Lord;
Envelop me within the cloud.
I'm coming up the mountain, Lord,
My heart unveiled before You
I will come.

I'm coming to worship,
I'm coming to bow down,
I'm coming to meet with You.

Matt Redman: Copyright © 1995 Kingsway's Thankyou Music, PO Box 75, Eastbourne, East Sussex, BN23 6NW, UK.
Psalm 24: 3,4. Exodus 33.

Friend of sinners, Lord of truth,
I am falling in love with You.
Friend of sinners, Lord of truth,
I have fallen in love with You.

Chorus:
Jesus, I love Your name,
The name by which we're saved.
Jesus, I love Your name,
The name by which we're saved.

Friend of sinners, Lord of truth,
I am giving my life to You,
Friend of sinners, Lord of truth,
I have given my life to You.

Matt Redman: Copyright © 1994 Kingsway's Thankyou Music, PO Box 75, Eastbourne, East Sussex, BN23 6NW, UK.

Chorus:
Fill us up and send us out
In the power of Your name,
Fill us up and send us out
In the power of Your name.

Have You not said
As we pass through water
You will be with us?
And You have said
When we walk through fire
We will not be burned.
We are not afraid, for You are with us,
We will testify
To the honour of Your name.
We are witnesses – You have shown us
You are the One who can save.

Bring them from the west,
Sons and daughters,
Call them for Your praise.
Gather from the east,
All Your children,
Coming home again.
Bring them from afar, all the nations,
From the north and south
Drawing all the peoples in.
Corners of the earth,
Come to see there's
Only one Saviour and King.

Chorus:
Fill us up and send us out
In the power of Your name.
Fill us up and send us out
In the power of Your name.

Matt Redman: Copyright © 1995 Kingsway's Thankyou Music, PO Box 75, Eastbourne, East Sussex, BN23 6NW, UK.
Acts 1:8, Isaiah 43.

How lovely is Your dwelling place,
O Lord Almighty.
My soul longs and even faints for You.
For here my heart is satisfied –
Within Your presence.
I sing beneath the shadow of
Your wings.

Chorus:
Better is one day in Your courts,
Better is one day in Your house,
Better is one day in Your courts
Than thousands elsewhere.

One thing I ask, and I would seek;
To see Your beauty:
To find You in the place
Your glory dwells.

Bridge:
My heart and flesh cry out
For You, the living God.
Your Spirit's water for my soul.
I've tasted and I've seen,
Come once again to me;
I will draw near to You,
I will draw near to You.

Matt Redman: Copyright © 1995 Kingsway's Thankyou Music, PO Box 75, Eastbourne, East Sussex, BN23 6NW, UK.
Psalm 84, Psalm 63, Psalm 27.

I have come to love You,
I have come to love You today.
I have come to love You,
I have come to love You today.

Chorus:
And today, and for evermore
I'll love Your name.
Lord, today, and for evermore
I'll love Your name.

I have come to worship,
I have come to worship today.
I have come to worship,
I have come to worship today.

I have come to thank You,
I have come to thank You today.
I have come to thank You,
I have come to thank You today.

Matt Redman: Copyright © 1995 Kingsway's Thankyou Music, PO Box 75, Eastbourne, East Sussex, BN23 6NW, UK.

I know Your arms are open wide, Father,
In I run with my whole life, and I,
Sing to You an offering,
The very best that I could bring,
You deserve much more than
I could give, for . . .

Chorus:
I'd never heard a sweeter voice,
Lord You made my aching heart rejoice.
Did angels in Your presence sing,
And all the courts of heaven ring . . .
When You called my name.
          (When You called my name).

It's like You whispered in my ear,
When You saved my soul
And brought me near, that now
I am found and I am Yours,
And true it's You my heart adores,
I cry out with all that is within, that . . .

Matt Redman: Copyright © 1994 Kingsway's Thankyou Music, PO Box 75, Eastbourne, East Sussex, BN23 6NW, UK.
Inspired by redemption hymns of W. Spencer Walton and D. Jenkins.

It's rising up, from coast to coast,
From north to south, and east to west,
The cry of hearts that love Your name,
Which with one voice we will proclaim.

The former things have taken place,
Can this be the new day of praise? –
A heavenly song that comes to birth
And reaches out to all the earth.
O, let the cry to nations ring,
That all may come and all may sing:

Holy is the Lord, Holy is the Lord.
Holy is the Lord, Holy is the Lord.

And we have heard the Lion's roar
That speaks of heaven's
Love and power,
Is this the time, is this the call
That ushers in Your kingdom rule?
O, let the cry to nations ring,
That all may come, and all may sing:

Jesus is alive,   Jesus is alive.
Jesus is alive,   Jesus is alive.

Matt Redman & Martin Smith: Copyright © 1995 Kingsway's Thankyou Music, PO Box 75, Eastbourne, East Sussex, BN23 6NW, UK.

I was a lost soul, captive to my history.
I stood ashamed of things
That had imprisoned me.
And then, up from the grave,
There rose one like the sun,
With healing in Your wings,
You turned my life around.

Chorus:
Sorrow may come, hardship rain down,
But rejoicing will shine in the morning.
You were there in the fast,
You are here in the feast,
Gone is my shame, here is dancing...
You've turned me around.

I live to thank the One
Who set me free from this,
You took a hurting life
And poured out tenderness.
You brought me from the depths,
And spared me from the pit,
You clothed me with Your joy,
And now my heart must sing.

I never thought I would see
The light that I've seen;
You have brought love and grace
And healing to me.
I never dreamt I could know the favour
I've known.
You heard my lonely cry
And made me Your own.

Matt Redman: Copyright © 1995 Kingsway's Thankyou Music, PO Box 75, Eastbourne, East Sussex, BN23 6NW, UK.
Psalm 30, Malachi 4:2.

I will offer up my life in spirit and truth,
Pouring out the oil of love
As my worship to You.
In surrender I must give my every part,
Lord, receive the sacrifice
Of a broken heart.

Chorus:
Jesus, what can I give,
What can I bring,
To so faithful a friend,
To so loving a king?
Saviour, what can be said,
What can be sung,
As a praise of Your name
For the things You have done?
O, my words could not tell,
Not even in part,
Of the debt of love that is owed
By this thankful heart.

You deserve my every breath,
For You've paid the great cost,
Giving up Your life to death,
Even death on a cross.
You took all my shame away,
There defeated my sin,
Opened up the gates of heaven,
And have beckoned me in.

Chorus:
Jesus, what can I give,
What can I bring,
To so faithful a friend,
To so loving a king?
Saviour, what can be said,
What can be sung,
As a praise of Your name
For the things You have done?
O, my words could not tell,
Not even in part,
Of the debt of love that is owed
By this thankful heart.

Jesus, is this song of love
Heard up in the heavens above?
Though I stumble and I stray,
Turn to me again.

Do not look upon my sin,
But, dear Lord, look deep within;
See the fire that burns therein –
Passion for Your name.

For even though You are a King,
I hear You call me as Your friend;
Is this a love that knows no bounds
And beckons even me?
And though Your name
Is greatly feared,
You still would draw a sinner near.
Turn, and with a gracious ear,
Hear my song of love.

Matt Redman: Copyright © 1995 Kingsway's Thankyou Music, PO Box 75, Eastbourne, East Sussex, BN23 6NW, UK.

Chorus:
Rags to riches is my song,
I had nothing in this world;
But You filled my empty cup,
And You healed my wayward soul.
Rags to riches is my song.

I cannot boast in worldly gain;
Like dust to dust it will soon fade away.
But I will boast in You alone,
Lord Jesus Christ, my wealth, my all.

A child of mercy I've become –
You're rich in love, and I was so poor.
All that seemed profit was but loss,
I've traded all for this pearl of price.

Matt Redman: Copyright © 1995 Kingsway's Thankyou Music, PO Box 75, Eastbourne, East Sussex, BN23 6NW, UK.
Phillipians 3:7, Romans 9:23, Matthew 6:21, Jeremiah 9:23,24.

The cross has said it all,
The cross has said it all.
I can't deny what You have shown,
The cross speaks of a God of love;
There displayed for all to see,
Jesus Christ, our only hope –
A message of the Father's heart,
"Come, my children, come on home."

Chorus:
As high as the heavens
Are above the earth,
So high is the measure
Of Your great love.
As far as the east is from the west,
So far have You taken our sins from us.

The cross has said it all,
The cross has said it all.
I never recognised Your touch,
Until I met You at the cross.
We are fallen, dust to dust,
How could You do this for us?
Son of God, shed precious blood,
Who can comprehend this love?

Chorus:
As high as the heavens
Are above the earth,
So high is the measure
Of Your great love.
As far as the east is from the west,
So far have You taken our sins from us.

How high, how wide, how deep.

Matt Redman and Martin Smith: Copyright © 1995 Kingsway's Thankyou Music, PO Box 75, Eastbourne, East Sussex, BN23 6NW, UK.
Psalm 103: 11,12, Ephesians 3:18.

This means I love You,
Singing this song;
Lord I don't have the words,
But I do have the will.
And this means I love You,
That I take up my cross,
I will sing as I walk out this love.

Chorus:
Jesus, this life is for You,
Everything, Lord, that I do;
Deeds that are pleasing
And ways that are pure,
Lord, may my life bear this fruit.

For these are the plans of my heart,
Yet often I'm missing the mark.
See my desire to live in Your truth –
This surely means I love You.

Matt Redman: Copyright © 1995 Kingsway's Thankyou Music, PO Box 75, Eastbourne, East Sussex, BN23 6NW, UK.

We've had a light shine in our midst,
We've felt Your presence,
We've known Your peace,
And though this blessing
Comes to us free
It carries a challenge to go.

We've had a feast laid on for us,
You have commanded
"Bring in the lost",
There's food for all, any who'd come,
Any who would know Your Son.

We know it's time to go,
We've heard the cries of all of the earth.
Send us with power,
We cannot do it alone.
With passion for the lost
We'll take the truth, whatever the cost;
Time is so short,
We cannot squander this love.

Chorus:
Surely the time has come
To bring the harvest home.
Surely the time has come
To bring the harvest home.

Matt Redman: Copyright © 1995 Kingsway's Thankyou Music, PO Box 75, Eastbourne, East Sussex, BN23 6NW, UK.